Simply Shrimp

Simply Shrimp

101 Recipes for Everybody's Favorite Seafood

by Rick Rodgers

Photographs by
Jennifer Lévy

CHRONICLE BOOKS
SAN FRANCISCO

Text copyright © 1998 by Rick Rodgers.

Photographs © 1998 by Jennifer Lévy.

Library of Congress Cataloging-in-Publication Data available.

ISBN 0-8118-1967-1

Printed in Hong Kong.

Food styling by Bettina Fisher.

Cover and interior design by Philip Krayna Design.

Distributed in Canada by Raincoast Books
8680 Cambie Street
Vancouver, British Columbia V6P 6M9

10 9 8 7 6 5 4 3 2 1

Chronicle Books
85 Second Street
San Francisco, California 94105

Web Site: www.chronbooks.com

Acknowledgments

It seems like such a cliché: "I want to thank so-and-so, without whom this book never would have been written." One thing I have learned in life is that clichés exist because they are usually facts.

This book grew from a conversation with Pat Adrian and Bill LeBlond about how shrimp has become a staple in today's kitchens. Thanks to both of them for their support, not only for this project, but through the years of our professional and personal relationships.

Ocean Garden Products in San Diego provided me with a generous amount of their excellent shrimp for testing recipes. Dixie Blake, director of marketing in San Diego, pulled the right strings, and Kevin Wank, at their distribution office in New Jersey, ensured our plans went smoothly. I am very grateful to them both.

All of my cookbooks have one common thread, my dear friend and associate Diane Kniss. We've lost track of how many recipes we've cooked together —probably because we were having so much fun we forgot to count! Also, thanks to Judith Dunbar Hines, another friend who believes in having a good time in the kitchen. And to Susan Ginsburg, my agent, a toast to many more years together in friendship and business.

Thanks to everyone at Chronicle Books who helped to make this book such a delight. Sarah Putman kept everything on track; Jennifer Lévy shot the gorgeous photos; Philip Krayna provided a spectacular design. Susan Derecskey is not only an excellent copy editor, but a good friend who generously gives welcome advice on how to make a book the best it can be.

Table of Contents

Introduction

When I was a caterer in Manhattan, there was one word guaranteed to sell a menu to an indecisive prospective client: shrimp.

Everyone loves shrimp. In fact, we eat more shrimp than any other fresh or frozen seafood. (Only canned tuna beats out shrimp in the seafood-per-capita competition.) We eat it fried into crisp, golden morsels, chilled in a tangy sauce, tucked into a sandwich or tortilla, simmered in a soup, tossed with pasta, spooned over rice, stir-fried with vegetables, or sizzling off the grill.

Thanks to modern processing and aquaculture techniques, shrimp is less expensive than ever before. Instead of buying in small amounts, you can now buy large bags of shrimp to store in the freezer and use as needed to create fast meals. Shrimp used to be reserved for special occasions, but nowadays, it is reasonably priced as well as fast-cooking and delicious.

As the cuisines of different countries are assimilated into our cuisine, we are discovering even more ways to enjoy shrimp. The intriguingly seasoned foods of Thailand, Vietnam, Malaysia, and Indonesia come to mind. Not that we don't have traditional shrimp recipes of our own. Think of Cajun spiced popcorn shrimp, shrimp boils from South Carolina and Maryland's Chesapeake Bay, California's shrimp Louis salad, and New Orleans shrimp rémoulade. Shrimp is complemented by many different ingredients, but certain fruits, vegetables, and seasonings are especially apt and show up often—artichokes, asparagus, zucchini, citrus and tropical fruits; ginger, dill, basil, tarragon, and cilantro. When choosing which recipes to include in this book, I decided to stick to familiar flavors that go comfortably together, rather than make strange culinary bedfellows in a display of virtuosity.

There's more good news for shrimp lovers! Shrimp is a lowfat food—less than 1 gram for a 1½-ounce serving. However, it is not low in cholesterol, so some people have been cautious about eating it too often. A recent study by Rockefeller University showed shrimp has a place in a heart-healthy diet. The test results showed an increase of good HDL cholesterol, which seems to retard the buildup of fatty deposits, with no increase of the LDL type. Also, the study's shrimp diet also lowered triglyceride levels, another factor that doctors look at when determining your heart health.

So, get ready to celebrate the chameleon of the kitchen—sensational shrimp!

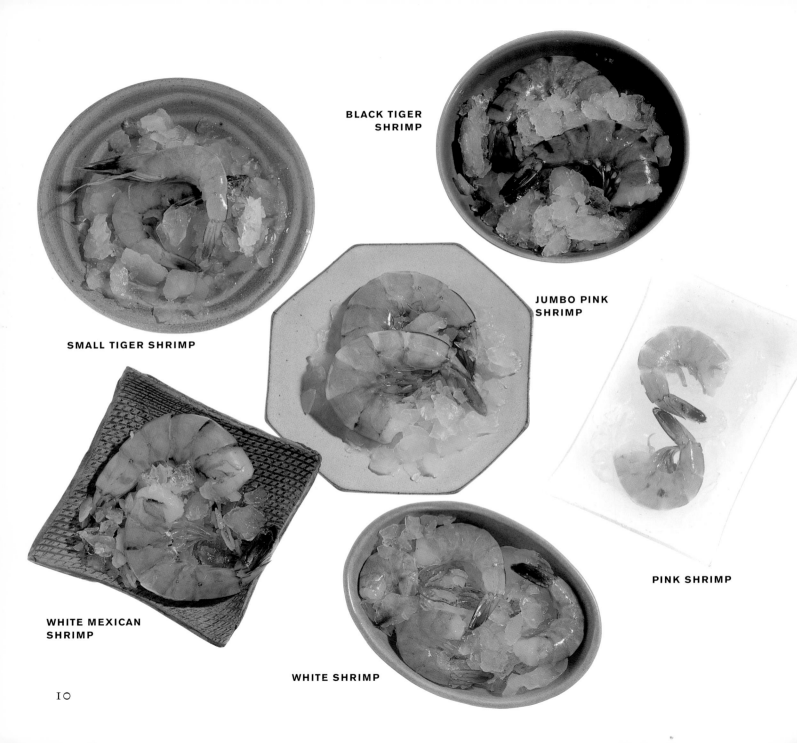

BLACK TIGER
SHRIMP

SMALL TIGER SHRIMP

JUMBO PINK
SHRIMP

PINK SHRIMP

WHITE MEXICAN
SHRIMP

WHITE SHRIMP

Sensational Shrimp

Literally thousands of shrimp species exist, but only 342 varieties have commercial value, and few of these have any impact on the market. Shrimp comes in different colors and sizes, sometimes fresh, and most likely frozen (in fact, frozen shrimp, properly thawed, is terrific). Knowing the differences between the various types of shrimp used to be moot, since the shopper was usually at the mercy of the local supermarket. But this is changing. New retail outlets for buying shrimp, such as price clubs and supermarket warehouses, are springing up. If you shop in an area with an Asian population, you could have a huge variety of shrimp to choose from (Asians are very particular about their seafood). Recently, while shopping at my favorite fishmarket in New York's Chinatown, I saw more than ten different kinds of thawed shrimp by the pound, plus six in frozen blocks. My local supermarket carries at least four different sizes of shrimp, peeled and unpeeled, plus tiny pink salad shrimp. Even if your supermarket or wholesale club doesn't offer much choice, it is still a good idea to be an educated shopper, and demand that your shrimp is as sweet-tasting as can be.

Types of Shrimp

The two major kinds of shrimp available in this country are **WARMWATER SHRIMP** and **COLDWATER SHRIMP**. Of the other two types, **FRESHWATER SHRIMP** can sometimes be found locally, and **SAND SHRIMP** are only popular in Europe. Shrimp is either wild-caught or farm-raised. Farm-raised shrimp has definitely made its mark. In 1982, only 2 percent was farm-raised. In 1992, that amount was twenty percent. Buy shrimp—and all shellfish—on the basis of flavor, not whether or not it was farm-raised.

WARMWATER SHRIMP: Warmwater shrimp is a tropical shellfish, and usually lives in warm, shallow water. It is the most commonly available shrimp. It is often categorized by shell colors: pink, white, blue, or black tiger. This can lead to some confusion, as the color differences are not always distinct to the eye.

White shrimp, the main shrimp variety consumed in this country, is available both wild and farm-raised, and many consider its crisp, juicy flesh to be unsurpassable. It is harvested in the Gulf of Mexico and along the coasts of Florida and the Carolinas.

You will also find farm-raised shrimp from China (with a somewhat flabby texture than benefits from a soaking in brine, described on page 15), India, and Ecuador.

Brown shrimp is very popular along the coast of Texas, where it is caught in the Gulf of Mexico. Brown shrimp has a briny, somewhat iodinelike flavor that comes from feeding on iodine-rich kelp.

Pink shrimp has a light pink shell and a sweet, rich flesh that some cooks think make it the best domestic shrimp available.

Black tiger shrimp is distinctive-looking, with a yellow-striped, midnight blue shell. It is rapidly becoming one of the most popular species for farm-raising and is generally less expensive than other tropical shrimp.

Rock shrimp, sometimes categorized as a coldwater shrimp, is caught along the Florida coast and some areas of California, like Santa Barbara. It gets its name from its tough, lobsterlike shell. Rock shrimp is sweet and plump. It can be used in any recipe that calls for peeled shrimp.

COLDWATER SHRIMP: This is most familiar as the ready-cooked, miniature shrimp tossed into salads and delicatessen sandwich filling.

Bay shrimp is also known as pink shrimp, tiny shrimp, baby shrimp, and salad shrimp. It inhabits the deep, frigid waters of the Pacific Northwest and Maine, as well as Scandinavia. It is the shrimp of choice for the San Francisco specialty, shrimp Louis salad.

Giant spot shrimp is found in the cold waters of the Pacific and Maine. It is usually marketed fresh—and it fetches a premium price at fine restaurants.

Shopping for Shrimp

SIZES: Shrimp is usually designated by size—large, medium, and jumbo are the most common sizes. But these designations change from city to city, and really don't mean much. The best way to buy shrimp is by the number of shrimp in a pound. For example, 31/35 shrimp has 31 to 35 shrimps to the pound. Huge shrimp is labeled U/12 or U/15, meaning under 12 or under 15 shrimp in a pound. Tiny shrimp can be marked OV/70 , for over seventy to a pound.

Choosing the right size shrimp depends on how you plan to cook it. The larger the shrimp, the less trouble it is to peel it. Jumbo shrimps are great on the grill, but it may be easier to eat medium or large shrimp in a pasta dish. Sometimes shrimp cooks more efficiently if each shrimp is cut lengthwise in half or is coarsely chopped. It's all a matter of common sense, so don't feel locked into sizes. If your fishmarket has medium-size shrimp on sale but your recipe calls for large shrimp, of course, the recipe will probably work with the smaller shrimps, so buy them. In this book I used mainly medium-size shrimp (36/40 shrimps to a pound) and large (which can be either 26/30 or 31/35, depending on the supermarket). The most popular designations, as arbitrary as they may seem, are on the following page. In many places, the word prawn has come to mean large-size shrimp. A true prawn, however, is a lobster-like crustacean, indigenous to European waters. Its full name is the Dublin Bay prawn; it is known as a *langoustine* in France, *scampi* in Venice, or *langostino* in the rest of Italy.

PREPARATION: Shrimp is now available in many different states of preparation, which is just one of the reasons for its increased popularity.

Block-frozen shrimp in 5-pound or 2-kilo (4.4-pound) frozen blocks can now be purchased in many markets, specially Asian, and wholesale clubs. Block-frozen shrimp is a very high quality product—the flavor, juices, color, and texture are frozen into the shrimp during processing, often right on the shrimp boats, to guarantee locked-in freshness. (It is usually the supermarket who messes up the shrimp by improper handling and storage.) Unless you live near a coastal community that has fresh shrimp, you are undoubtedly purchasing thawed shrimp at your market.

The best way to thaw a block of frozen shrimp is in the refrigerator, which will take 24 to 48 hours. However, most restaurants and fishmarkets simply thaw the easy way—placing the block of shrimp under cold running water until the shrimp can be separated from each other. Be sure to use *cold* water, not warm or hot, as the warmer water could start to cook the shrimp. Never thaw a block of shrimp in a microwave

Shrimp Sizes	
U/12	Super-colossal
U/15	Colossal
16/20	Super-jumbo
21/25	Jumbo
26/30	Extra-large
31/35	Large
36/40	Medium
40+	Cocktail or salad

(the ends of the block will cook while the middle stays frozen) or by allowing it to stand in a warm place (which invites bacterial growth).

If you know that you will not be eating all of the shrimp at once, only thaw it until you can separate the shrimp from the block. Continue to rinse and thaw the shrimp you will be cooking immediately; it can be refrigerated for up to two days. Rewrap (first in plastic wrap, then foil) and refreeze the remaining, partially frozen shrimp block and use within two months.

IQF, or individually quick frozen, shrimp is a fairly recent development. The shrimp is not frozen into a block but processed separately and stored in bags. You just take out what you need, thaw, and cook. Be careful when storing IQF shrimp, as individual shrimps can break easily if jostled. Use within two months, since home freezers don't have the subzero temperatures of commercial freezers, and even frozen foods don't last indefinitely.

P & D, or peeled and deveined, shrimp is becoming more common. While they have less flavor than shell-on shrimps, since juices are lost in processing, they certainly save time when you are cooking for a crowd. Peeled but undeveined shrimps are called PUD, or puds. Another category is E-Z Peel, where the deveining incision makes it easy to pull off the shell.

Cooked shrimp is also available, and it is a convenience, but you have to weigh the loss of flavor against the time saved. (Tiny pink coldwater shrimp is available only cooked.) When you want to serve a mountain of shrimp with dip for Super Bowl, cooked shrimp is the way to go.

Headless shrimp, also known as green headless shrimp, is with the heads removed, but the shell still on, uncooked. (To a shrimp purveyor, "green" has nothing to do with color but refers to raw shrimp.) Headless shrimp can also be purchased shelled, or peeled.

Whole shrimp is becoming more available, especially since Asian consumers ask for them. Dramatic-looking whole shrimp is also very popular at upscale restaurants. Some cooks twist off the shrimp heads and turn them into a rich stock. Others cook the whole shrimp and remove the heads at the table. Cook whole shrimps on the day of purchase; they are more perishable than headless shrimp. When the heads are removed, there is at least 35 percent loss, so purchase at least one third more than you would if buying regular headless shrimp (1 pound, 6 ounces whole shrimp to get one pound headless).

FRESHNESS: Shrimp should have a clean, fresh aroma, like an ocean breeze. Whenever possible, smell the shrimp before buying it. If you are allowed to touch the shrimp, it should feel somewhat firm, and not mushy.

Thawed shrimp should be kept as cold as possible for the longest storage life, which will be two days at most. The best way is to put the shrimp in a large self-sealing plastic bag. Place the bag of shrimp on a bed of ice cubes in a bowl or baking dish in the refrigerator. Replace the ice cubes as they melt.

Preparing Shrimp

PEELING SHRIMP: Many shrimp peeling gadgets are sold in housewares stores, but I have found none more efficient than a pair of hands. Just peel each shrimp from the underside, where the feelers are. Some recipes call for leaving the tail segment on, so the tail becomes a natural holder for dipping. For super-size shrimp, use kitchen shears to snip down the back of each shrimp. This will also reveal the intestinal vein, which you can remove, if you wish.

Never throw away shrimp peels! They can be turned into a versatile stock (see page 16). If necessary, tuck them into a plastic bag and freeze to simmer into stock at another time.

DEVEINING SHRIMP: Once the shrimps have been peeled you have to decide whether to devein or not. Shrimps have an intestinal vein than runs down the back. If it is thick, visible, and black, especially in super-size shrimp, remove it. If it is thin and white, don't bother. If you are serving shrimp with the shell on, you can, if you wish, devein through the shell or leave it up to the individual to devein at the table.

The main thing to remember is that there is nothing in the vein that will harm you.

To devein a shrimp, run a small, sharp knife along the back of the shrimp to make a shallow incision. Working under a thin stream of cold running water, lift out the vein with the tip of the knife. Pat the shrimp dry with paper towels.

BRINING SHRIMP: When dealing with shrimp from an unfamiliar source, it is a good idea to sauté or boil one shrimp to taste and judge its flavor and texture. If it seems a little flabby, soak the shrimp in a brine. The brine will draw out excess moisture and help firm the flesh.

To make the brine, dissolve 1 cup salt (preferably sea salt, but table salt will do) and ½ cup sugar in 2 cups boiling water. Transfer to a large bowl, add 2 trays of ice water, and cool. Stir in the shrimp and refrigerate for 1 hour. If brining peeled shrimp, let stand for only 30 minutes. Drain, rinse, and pat dry.

If the shrimp has an iodine taste, make a solution of 2 tablespoons baking soda dissolved in 4 quarts cold water. Soak the shrimp for 10 minutes only. Drain, rinse very well, and pat dry.

Shells (and heads, if available) from
   1 to 2 pounds of shrimp

1 cup bottled clam juice, canned low-
   sodium chicken broth, or additional
   water

1 small onion, chopped

1 small celery rib with leaves, chopped

2 sprigs of fresh parsley

⅛ teaspoon dried thyme

4 whole peppercorns

¼ teaspoon salt

MAKES ABOUT 4 CUPS

Shrimp Stock

Shrimp shells can be transformed, practically without effort, into a useful stock. For a stock with a fuller flavor, use bottled clam juice or canned chicken broth as part of the liquid—the shells from only one pound of shrimp may need a little help. Of course, if you have homemade fish or chicken stock on hand, so much the better.

IN A MEDIUM SAUCEPAN, combine the shrimp shells, 4 cups water, clam juice, onion, and celery. Bring to a boil over high heat, skimming off any foam that rises to the surface. Add the parsley, thyme, and peppercorns. Reduce the heat to low and simmer for at least 15 and up to 30 minutes. Season with the salt.

STRAIN THE STOCK THROUGH A WIRE SIEVE, pressing hard on the shells to extract all of the stock. (The stock can be prepared up to 1 day ahead, cooled completely, covered, and refrigerated; it can be frozen for up to 1 month.)

ASIAN SHRIMP STOCK:
Substitute 1 scallion, white and green parts, coarsely chopped for the onion. Add ⅓ cup dry sherry, 2 quarter-size slices fresh ginger, and 1 garlic clove, crushed. Omit the parsley and thyme.

MEDITERRANEAN SHRIMP STOCK:
Substitute ½ cup dry white wine or dry vermouth for ½ cup of the water.

SHRIMP STOCK WITH CORIANDER:
Add 2 teaspoons whole coriander seeds to the stock with the peppercorns.

Basic Cooked Shrimp

Some recipes in this book call for "cooked, peeled, and deveined" shrimp. The flavor of freshly cooked shrimp is superior to precooked shrimp. In some recipes, when the shrimp cooking liquid is used as an ingredient, I have included the precooking as a step in the recipe. Otherwise, this is the recipe to use. If you wish, you can flavor the cooking water with onion, bay leaf, and a few peppercorns.

1 pound shrimp

½ teaspoon salt

1 small onion, sliced (optional)

1 bay leaf (optional)

4 whole peppercorns (optional)

MAKES 1 POUND SHRIMP

IN A MEDIUM SAUCEPAN, bring 4 cups water and the salt to a boil over high heat. Add the shrimp. Cook until the shrimps turn pink, opaque, and firm, 2 to 3 minutes, counting from the time you add the shrimp. (The water does not have to return to a boil.) Drain and rinse under cold running water until easy to handle. Peel and devein the shrimps.

Appetizing Shrimp

Fearless Frying
New-Fashioned Shrimp Cocktail Martini with Celery Vinaigrette
Salsa Shrimp Cocktail with Tortilla Crisps
Shrimp Rémoulade with Beefsteak Tomatoes
Shrimp, Mozzarella, and Sun-Dried Tomato Quesadillas
Coconut Shrimp with Easy Peanut Sauce
Shrimp and Corn Fritters
Caribbean Shrimp and Potato Balls
Popcorn Shrimp with Shocking Pink Sauce
Beer-Batter Shrimp with Hot-and-Sweet Mustard Dip
Shrimp Tempura with Ginger Dipping Sauce
Filipino Shrimp and Sweet Potato Pancakes with Garlic Sauce
Shrimp Pot Stickers
Shrimp con Queso
Baked Shrimp Spring Rolls
Cilantro Shrimp Toasts
Shrimp Seviche with Grapefruit-Avocado Salsa
Scandinavian Vodka-Soused Shrimp
Pickled Picnic Shrimp
Potted Shrimp with Dill and Dijon Mustard
Crostini with Shrimp, Capers, and Olives
Shrimp and Roasted Red Pepper Mini Wraps
New Orleans Shrimp and Artichoke Terrine

Fearless Frying

Few cooking techniques give the irresistible crunch of deep-frying. Crisp food is a great appetite-teaser, so it's no wonder so many popular appetizers are deep-fried. Here are a few tips to guarantee perfect deep-frying results.

THE RIGHT POT: An electric deep-fryer (often one of the features of a multi-cooker that also stews and slow-cooks) is great, because it has a thermostat to help control the heat of the oil. A large, heavy saucepan (preferably cast-iron) on the stove will also work, as long as you attach a deep-fry thermometer. A good deep-frying thermometer is essential. It should have a clip so it can be attached to the side of the pan. Be sure the thermometer's bulb (or tip) is submerged by at least 1 inch in the fat to get an accurate temperature reading.

Skillets are not right for every deep-frying job. Some foods need to swim in the fat to cook properly, and a skillet just isn't deep enough. It is also hard to gauge the temperature, since a deep-fry thermometer won't stand up in the pan. An electric skillet, however, works well for some smaller foods.

THE RIGHT TEMPERATURE: The trick with deep-frying is to pick a temperature that allows the outside of the food to become crisp in the same length of time that it takes to cook through. Higher oil temperatures (360° to 375° F.) seal the exterior, keeping the juices inside. If the oil temperature is too low, the food can soak up the oil, giving soggy, greasy results. The best way to test the oil temperature in a stovetop skillet is by the old bread cube test. If a cube of bread cooks to golden brown in about a minute, the temperature of the oil is from 360° to 375° F., the magic range for deep-frying shrimp.

THE RIGHT FAT: Vegetable shortening is a better choice for deep-frying than vegetable oil. Since shortening is more highly processed than oil, it releases less odor into the air. Always use enough fat to do the job efficiently: Melt enough shortening over medium-high heat to come at least two inches up the sides of the pan (or at least one inch in a skillet). Depending on the recipe, you will need at least two pounds of shortening. Don't worry about straining the fat and saving it for another deep-frying job—just factor the cost of the shortening into the cost of the dish. Most cooks don't deep-fry so often that saving the shortening should be a concern.

NO CROWDING: Never crowd food while deep-frying, or it will give off steam which discourages crisping. When deep-frying in batches, let the fat return to its original temperature before frying another batch. Use a skimmer or slotted spoon to lift the food out of the fat. The best place to drain deep-fried foods is on a wire cake rack set over a rimmed baking sheet. The wire rack is a better solution than paper towel or paper bags because where the food touches the paper, steam collects under the surface and eventually moistens the crust.

NO WAITING: Deep-fried foods don't like to wait around: serve them as soon as you can. If necessary, keep the food warm in a low (200° F.) oven for a few minutes until you have finished deep-frying the second batch and are ready to serve. Whenever possible, serve each batch as soon as it comes out of the pan, instead of frying up all of the food and keeping it warm. It only takes a few minutes to fry each batch, and you will be serving the food at its best.

CELERY VINAIGRETTE

5 large celery ribs with leaves, cut into ¼-inch dice

¼ cup vegetable oil

2 tablespoons fresh lemon juice

2 tablespoons finely chopped fresh parsley

¼ teaspoon salt

¼ teaspoon freshly ground pepper

COCKTAIL SAUCE

1 cup prepared American-style chili sauce

1 small celery rib with leaves, minced

1 tablespoon prepared horseradish

1 tablespoon fresh lemon juice

1 tablespoon finely chopped fresh parsley

1 tablespoon vodka or gin (optional)

36 large shrimp (about 1½ pounds), cooked, peeled with the tail segment left on and deveined (page 17)

MAKES 6 SERVINGS

New-Fashioned Shrimp Cocktail Martini with Celery Vinaigrette

Truly a classic of American cuisine, the shrimp cocktail has been cruelly misrepresented, especially in little glass jars at the supermarket. This updated version gets a snappy presentation in a chilled martini glass—add a jolt of vodka or gin to the sauce, if you like—and is served on a bed of crunchy chopped celery salad.

TO MAKE THE CELERY VINAIGRETTE, combine all of the ingredients in a medium bowl. Cover and refrigerate until chilled, at least 2 hours or overnight.

TO MAKE THE COCKTAIL SAUCE, combine all of the ingredients in a small bowl. Cover and refrigerate until chilled and the flavors are blended, at least 2 hours or overnight.

TO SERVE, PLACE 4 MARTINI GLASSES in the freezer for 10 minutes to chill. Using a slotted spoon, place equal portions of the celery vinaigrette in the martini glasses. Hook 6 shrimps in a circle around the edge of each glass, tails facing out. Spoon about 3 tablespoons of the Cocktail Sauce into the center of each glass. Serve chilled.

Salsa Shrimp Cocktail with Tortilla Crisps

This south-of-the-border version of the classic shrimp cocktail gets its heat from chile peppers instead of horseradish. Serve it in balloon wine, coupe, or martini glasses.

TO MAKE THE SALSA, combine all of the ingredients in a medium bowl. Cover and refrigerate until chilled and the flavors are blended, at least 2 hours or overnight.

TO SERVE, PLACE 4 WIDE GLASSES in the freezer for 10 minutes to chill. Layer equal portions of salsa and chopped shrimp into the glasses. Stand the tortilla crisps up in the salsa and serve chilled.

Tortilla Crisps

Cut 2 corn tortillas (6 inches) into long, ¼- to ½-inch-wide strips or freeform shapes, such as zigzags. In a large, heavy skillet, melt enough vegetable shortening over medium-high heat to come ½ inch up the sides. Heat the shortening until very hot but not smoking. Fry the tortilla shapes until crisp and golden brown, about 1 minute. Using a skimmer, transfer to a wire cake rack or paper towels to drain and cool.

SALSA

1 pound ripe plum tomatoes, seeded and cut into ¼-inch dice

3 tablespoons minced red onion

3 tablespoons fresh lime juice

2 tablespoons finely chopped fresh cilantro

1 jalapeño, seeded and minced

2 garlic cloves, crushed through a press

½ teaspoon salt

24 cooked large shrimp (about 1 pound) preferably cooked Beer and Spiced Shrimp (page 77) or Basic Cooked Shrimp (page 17), peeled deveined, and coarsely chopped

Tortilla Crisps (recipe follows) or tortilla chips, for garnish

MAKES 4 SERVINGS

½ cup mayonnaise

1 tablespoon Creole Mustard (see Note)

1 tablespoon catsup

⅓ cup minced celery rib with leaves

1 tablespoon minced shallot

1½ teaspoons prepared horseradish

1 small garlic clove, crushed through a press

1 teaspoon mustard seeds

½ teaspoon whole peppercorns

½ teaspoon salt

1½ pounds medium shrimp, unpeeled

6 large beefsteak tomatoes, cut crosswise into ¼-inch-thick slices

MAKES 6 SERVINGS

Shrimp Rémoulade with Beefsteak Tomatoes

Shrimp rémoulade is a mainstay of just about every restaurant in New Orleans. It gets its name from the French Picard dialect word for horseradish, *ramolas*. The original recipe must have been very hot, but modern versions just include a hint of horseradish, or even omit it entirely. Shrimp rémoulade and juicy beefsteak tomatoes are a sensational combination.

TO MAKE THE SAUCE, combine all of the ingredients in a small bowl. Cover and refrigerate for at least 1 hour or overnight.

IN A LARGE SAUCEPAN, bring 6 cups of water, the mustard seeds, peppercorns, and salt to a boil over high heat. Add the shrimp and cook just until pink and firm, 2 to 3 minutes (the water does not need to return to a boil). Drain and rinse under cold water until easy to handle. Peel and devein. In a medium bowl, combine the peeled shrimps and the Rémoulade Sauce. Cover and refrigerate until chilled, at least 1 hour or overnight.

TO SERVE, MAKE CIRCLES OF OVERLAPPING TOMATO SLICES on 6 dinner plates. Spoon the shrimp into the centers of the tomato circles. Serve chilled.

NOTE: Creole mustard is especially spicy. Zatarain's is a popular brand. It is available at many supermarkets and specialty food stores. Spicy brown mustard is a good substitute.

Shrimp, Mozzarella, and Sun-Dried Tomato Quesadillas

Quesadillas are certainly Mexican, but they lend themselves to the flavors of other nations, like this Italian "formaggio-dilla."

PREHEAT THE OVEN TO 200° F.

HEAT A MEDIUM SKILLET OVER MEDIUM HEAT. Place 1 tortilla in the skillet. Sprinkle with one fourth each of the mozzarella, shrimp, tomatoes, and basil. Cook until the cheese begins to melt and the underside of the tortilla is marked with browned spots, about 1½ minutes. Place another tortilla on top and press lightly. Turn the quesadilla and continue cooking until the cheese is melted and the second side is spotted with brown, about 1 minute. Transfer to a baking sheet and keep warm in the oven. Repeat with the remaining ingredients. Cut the quesadillas into wedges and serve warm.

8 flour tortillas (8 inches)

2 cups shredded mozzarella cheese

8 ounces medium shrimp, cooked, peeled, and deveined (see page 17)

½ cup chopped sun-dried tomatoes packed in oil

¼ cup chopped fresh basil or 1 teaspoon dried oregano

MAKES 6 TO 8 SERVINGS

Coconut Shrimp with Easy Peanut Sauce

When I was a teenager in San Francisco, a sophisticated date meant a trip to the Tonga Room in the Fairmont Hotel. They specialized in "Polynesian" pu-pu platters, and coconut shrimp was a favorite. I still make it as a special treat, but in a less-sweet contemporary version served with a Thai-inspired peanut sauce dip.

TO MAKE THE SAUCE, whisk all of the ingredients in a small bowl and set aside. (The sauce can be prepared up to 2 hours ahead, covered, and kept at room temperature. If the sauce thickens upon standing, thin to a thick dipping consistency with broth or water.)

TO MAKE THE BATTER, in a medium bowl, whisk the flour, baking powder, curry powder, salt, and cayenne to mix. Add the beer and eggs and stir with a spoon just until combined (do not overmix). Fold in ½ cup of the coconut. Place the remaining coconut on a plate.

PREHEAT THE OVEN TO 200° F. Place a wire cake rack over a jelly-roll pan.

IN A LARGE, HEAVY SAUCEPAN, melt enough vegetable shortening over medium-high heat to come 3 inches up the sides of the pan and heat to 360° F. Working in batches, dip the shrimps, one at a time, in the batter, then roll them in the coconut. Deep-fry until golden, 2 to 3 minutes. Using a slotted skimmer, transfer the shrimps to the wire rack and keep warm in the oven. Repeat with the remaining shrimps, batter, and coconut, allowing the shortening to return to 360° F. before frying each batch. Serve immediately, with the peanut sauce for dipping.

EASY PEANUT SAUCE

- ⅓ cup chicken broth, preferably home-made, or use low-sodium canned broth
- ¼ cup unsalted peanut butter
- ¼ cup hoisin sauce
- 1 tablespoon Asian fish sauce (see page 37)

COCONUT BATTER

- 1 cup all-purpose flour
- 1 teaspoon baking powder
- 1½ teaspoons Madras-style curry powder
- ½ teaspoon salt
- ⅛ teaspoon cayenne
- 1¼ cups flat lager beer
- 2 large eggs, beaten
- 1 cup unsweetened desiccated coconut (available at natural food stores)

- 1 pound extra-large to large shrimp, peeled with the tail segment left on and deveined
- Vegetable shortening, for deep-frying

MAKES 6 TO 8 SERVINGS

1 cup all-purpose flour

½ cup corn flour (see Note)

¾ teaspoon baking soda

¾ teaspoon salt

½ teaspoon onion powder

¼ teaspoon garlic powder

1 cup buttermilk

1 large egg, beaten

8 ounces small shrimp, peeled, deveined, and coarsely chopped

1 cup fresh or thawed frozen corn kernels

Vegetable shortening, for deep-frying

Rémoulade Sauce, Cocktail Sauce, or Shocking Pink Sauce (pages 24, 22, and 30), for dipping

MAKES ABOUT 24 FRITTERS

Shrimp and Corn Fritters

Serve these light, golden puffs with your favorite dip—I'm partial to the Rémoulade Sauce (page 24).

IN A MEDIUM BOWL, whisk the flour, corn flour, baking soda, salt, onion powder, and garlic powder to mix. Add the buttermilk and egg and stir with a spoon just until blended (do not overmix). Fold in the shrimp and corn.

PREHEAT THE OVEN TO 200° F. Place a wire cake rack over a jelly-roll pan.

IN A LARGE, HEAVY SAUCEPAN, melt enough vegetable shortening over medium-high heat to come 3 inches up the sides of the pan and heat to 360° F. Working in batches, drop the batter by the tablespoonful into the hot shortening. Deep-fry until golden brown, turning once, 3 to 4 minutes. Using a slotted skimmer, transfer the fritters to the cake rack and keep warm in the oven. Repeat with the remaining batter, allowing the shortening to return to 360° F. before frying each batch. Serve warm, with the sauce for dipping.

NOTE: Corn flour is a finely ground cornmeal with a powdery texture. It is often sold in Southern markets as "fish fry." To make your own, process stoneground yellow cornmeal in a blender until floury, 1 to 2 minutes. You may have to stop the blender occasionally and use a chopstick to loosen the collected flour from around the blades.

Caribbean Shrimp and Potato Balls

Pickapeppa sauce is a complex spiced condiment found in specialty stores and many supermarkets. It makes a great dip for these crisp cheese balls studded with chopped shrimp.

IN A MEDIUM SAUCEPAN OF LIGHTLY SALTED WATER, cook the potato until tender when pierced with the tip of a sharp knife, about 30 minutes. Cool and peel the potato. Place in a medium bowl and mash until smooth.

MEANWHILE, IN A MEDIUM NONSTICK SKILLET, heat the oil over medium heat. Add the scallions, ginger, and garlic and stir until the scallions wilt, about 1 minute. Add the shrimp and cook until pink and firm, 1 to 2 minutes. Transfer to the bowl with the potatoes. Mix in the cheddar, egg yolk, Pickapeppa sauce, salt, and pepper. Cover and refrigerate until chilled, about 1 hour.

HAVE READY 3 SHALLOW DISHES, one with the flour, one with the beaten eggs, and one with the bread crumbs. Rinse your hands with water and form the potato mixture into balls, using 1 tablespoon for each. Roll each ball in the flour, dip in the eggs, and roll in the bread crumbs. Place on a wax paper–lined baking sheet. Refrigerate, uncovered, to set the breading, at least 1 hour and up to 8 hours.

PREHEAT THE OVEN TO 200° F. Place a wire cake rack over a jelly roll pan.

IN A LARGE, HEAVY SAUCEPAN, melt enough vegetable shortening over medium-high heat to come 3 inches up the sides of the pan and heat to 360° F. Working in batches without crowding, deep-fry the balls until golden brown, about 3 minutes. Using a slotted skimmer, transfer to the wire rack and keep warm in the oven. Repeat with the remaining batter, allowing the shortening to return to 360° F. before frying each batch. Serve warm, with a small bowl of the Pickapeppa sauce for dipping.

1 large (8 ounces) baking potato, scrubbed

1 tablespoon vegetable oil

2 scallions, white and green parts, finely chopped

1 tablespoon minced fresh ginger

1 garlic clove, minced

8 ounces medium shrimp, peeled, deveined, and coarsely chopped

1 cup shredded sharp cheddar cheese

1 large egg yolk

1 teaspoon Pickapeppa sauce, plus more for dipping

½ teaspoon salt

¼ teaspoon freshly ground pepper

2 large eggs, beaten

1 cup all-purpose flour

1½ cups fresh bread crumbs

Vegetable shortening, for deep-frying

MAKES ABOUT 22 BALLS

Popcorn Shrimp with Shocking Pink Sauce

Is this called popcorn shrimp because the little shrimps look like popped corn kernels, or because they have a golden coating of corn flour, or because people can eat them by the handful? Make this with the smallest shrimp you can find to play up the popcorn look. Be careful not to fry the shrimps until golden brown, or they will be overcooked.

SHOCKING PINK SAUCE

½ cup mayonnaise

2 tablespoons catsup

1 tablespoon coarse-grain mustard

1 tablespoon prepared horseradish

1 tablespoon bottled capers, rinsed and coarsely chopped if large

1 tablespoon minced shallot or scallion, white part only

1 tablespoon chopped fresh parsley

½ teaspoon hot red pepper sauce, or to taste

4 large eggs

½ teaspoon salt

¼ teaspoon hot red pepper sauce

2 pounds small shrimp, peeled and deveined

1 cup corn flour (see Note page 28)

Vegetable shortening, for deep-frying

MAKES 4 TO 6 SERVINGS

TO MAKE THE SAUCE, combine all of the ingredients in a small bowl. Cover and refrigerate for at least 1 hour.

PLACE A LARGE WIRE CAKE RACK over a jelly-roll pan. In a medium bowl, beat the eggs, salt, and hot pepper sauce. Have the corn flour in another medium bowl. One at a time, drop the shrimps into the beaten eggs, then roll in the corn flour. Transfer to the cake rack. (Using one hand for dipping into the egg and the other for rolling in the flour helps them from getting as coated as the shrimps.) Refrigerate, uncovered, to set the breading, at least 30 minutes and up to 1 hour. Remove the shrimps from the rack and place on a baking sheet.

PREHEAT THE OVEN TO 200° F.

IN A LARGE, HEAVY SAUCEPAN, melt enough vegetable shortening over medium-high heat to come 3 inches up the sides and heat to 375° F. Working in batches without crowding, deep-fry the shrimps just until golden, about 2 minutes. Transfer the shrimps to the cake rack to drain, and keep warm in the oven while deep-frying the remaining ones. Serve immediately with the sauce for dipping.

Beer-Batter Shrimp with Hot-and-Sweet Mustard Dip

The yeasts in beer work with the leavening power of baking powder to make a fluffy, crisp shrimp coating. Open up a mild-flavored beer, such as lager, and let it stand at room temperature for an hour or so to get flat before making the batter.

TO MAKE THE DIP, in a small bowl, mix the mustard and honey. (The dip can be prepared up to 3 days ahead, covered, and refrigerated. Serve at room temperature.)

TO MAKE THE BATTER, in a medium bowl, whisk the flour, baking powder, salt, and cayenne to mix. Add the beer and eggs and stir with a spoon just until combined (do not overmix).

PREHEAT THE OVEN TO 200° F. Place a wire cake rack over a jelly-roll pan.

IN A LARGE, DEEP, HEAVY SAUCEPAN, melt enough vegetable shortening over medium-high heat to come 3 inches up the sides of the pan and heat to 360° F. Working in batches, dip the shrimps, one at a time, in the batter. Deep-fry until golden, about 2 minutes. Using a slotted skimmer, transfer the shrimps to the wire rack and keep warm in the oven. Repeat with the remaining shrimps and batter, allowing the shortening to return to 360° F. before frying each batch. If the batter thickens upon standing, thin with a little beer. Serve immediately, with the mustard dip.

HOT-AND-SWEET MUSTARD DIP

⅓ cup prepared Chinese mustard

⅓ cup honey

BEER BATTER

1 cup all-purpose flour

1 teaspoon baking powder

½ teaspoon salt

⅛ teaspoon cayenne

1¼ cups flat lager beer

2 large eggs, beaten

1 pound large shrimp, peeled with the tail segment left on and deveined

Vegetable shortening, for deep-frying

MAKES 4 TO 6 SERVINGS

GINGER DIPPING SAUCE

¼ cup shredded fresh ginger (use the large holes of a cheese grater)

¼ cup soy sauce, preferably Japanese

¼ cup sweet sherry, such as oloroso

¼ cup rice vinegar

1 tablespoon light brown sugar

1 cup white rice flour (available at Asian markets or natural food stores) or cake flour (not self-rising)

¼ teaspoon baking powder

¾ cup ice water

1 large egg, beaten

Vegetable shortening, for deep-frying

1 pound medium shrimp, peeled (leave tail segment attached) and deveined

MAKES 4 SERVINGS

Shrimp Tempura with Ginger Dipping Sauce

Looking for the lightest tempura batter of all? Use rice flour, which has no gluten (gluten is the protein in wheat flour that gives a dough structure and strength).

TO MAKE THE SAUCE, place the ginger in the corner of a clean kitchen towel. Squeeze and wring the ginger over a small bowl to extract the juice; discard the pulp. You should have 2 tablespoons ginger juice.

IN A SMALL, NONREACTIVE SAUCEPAN, bring the soy sauce, sherry, vinegar, and sugar to a boil over high heat. Cook for 1 minute. Cool completely. Stir in the ginger juice. Set aside.

TO MAKE THE BATTER, in a medium bowl, whisk the rice flour and baking powder to mix. Add the water and beaten egg. Stir with a spoon just until combined (do not overmix).

PREHEAT THE OVEN TO 200° F. Place a wire cake rack over a jelly-roll pan.

IN A LARGE, HEAVY SAUCEPAN, melt enough vegetable shortening over medium-high heat to come 3 inches up the sides of the pan and heat to 375° F. Working in batches, dip the shrimps, one at a time, in the batter. Deep-fry until golden, 2 to 3 minutes. Using a slotted skimmer, transfer the shrimps to the wire rack and keep warm in the oven. Repeat with the remaining shrimps and batter, allowing the shortening to return to 375° F. before frying each batch. If the batter thickens upon standing, thin with a little water. Serve immediately, with the dipping sauce.

Filipino Shrimp and Sweet Potato Pancakes with Garlic Sauce

The combination of shrimp and sweet potatoes is uncommon, but Filipino cooks know a good match when they see it. For the most flavorful results, use an orange-fleshed sweet potato, often called a yam, not the pale variety. These unusual pancakes are versatile—they can be served cut into quarters as finger food or left whole to serve on a plate as an appetizer or even as a light main course.

TO MAKE THE SAUCE, in a small bowl, combine all the ingredients. Cover and set aside.

POSITION A RACK IN THE CENTER OF THE OVEN and preheat to 200° F.

IN A MEDIUM BOWL, whisk the flour, cornstarch, salt, and pepper to mix. Add the egg and ½ cup water and stir just to combine. Fold in the sweet potato, shrimp and half of the scallions.

IN A LARGE (12-INCH) SKILLET, heat the oil over medium-high heat. Working in batches, pour the batter by the ⅓ cup into the skillet, spreading out the batter to form 4-inch-wide pancakes. Sprinkle the tops of the pancakes with the remaining scallions. Cook until browned on both sides, turning once, 3 to 4 minutes total. Transfer to a baking sheet and keep warm while making the remaining pancakes, adding more oil to the skillet as needed. Serve warm, with the Garlic Sauce for dipping.

GARLIC SAUCE

- ½ cup distilled white vinegar
- 3 garlic cloves, minced
- 1 teaspoon sugar, preferably superfine
- ¼ teaspoon salt

- ½ cup all-purpose flour
- ½ cup cornstarch
- ¼ teaspoon salt
- ¼ teaspoon freshly ground pepper
- 1 large egg, beaten
- 1 large (12 ounces) sweet potato, peeled and coarsely shredded
- 8 ounces medium shrimp, peeled, deveined, and cut lengthwise in half
- 4 scallions, white and green parts, finely chopped
- 2 tablespoons vegetable oil, plus more as needed

MAKES 8 PANCAKES

¾ pound medium shrimp, peeled, deveined, and finely chopped

1¼ cups packed finely chopped napa cabbage

3 tablespoons finely chopped scallions, white and green parts

1 tablespoon minced fresh ginger

1 large garlic clove, minced

1½ tablespoons soy sauce

1½ tablespoons dry sherry

¼ teaspoon sugar

¼ teaspoon salt

Cornstarch, for dusting

24 round won ton or gyoza wrappers

2 tablespoons vegetable oil

¾ cup chicken broth, preferably home-made, or use low-sodium canned broth

DIPPING SAUCE

¼ cup soy sauce

2 tablespoons rice vinegar

1 teaspoon hot chili oil (see Note)

MAKES ABOUT 24 POT STICKERS

Shrimp Pot Stickers

I know that these are supposed to be appetizers, but I often make them for dinner, accompanied by a cucumber salad dressed with rice vinegar and sesame oil.

IN A MEDIUM BOWL, mix the shrimp, cabbage, scallions, ginger, garlic, soy sauce, sherry, sugar, and salt.

LIGHTLY DUST A BAKING SHEET with cornstarch. Place 1 tablespoon of the mixture in the center of 1 wrapper. Brush the edges of the wrapper with cold water. Bring the edges of the wrapper up to meet in the center above the filling. Pinch and pleat the edges of the wrapper closed. Transfer to the baking sheet. Repeat with the remaining wrappers and filling.

IN A LARGE (12-INCH) NONSTICK SKILLET, heat the oil over high heat until very hot but not smoking. Add the dumplings, and reduce the heat to medium. Cook until the undersides are browned, about 2 minutes. Add the broth and bring to a boil over medium-high heat. Partially cover the skillet and boil until the broth is almost evaporated, about 6 minutes. Remove the cover and boil until the broth evaporates completely and the pot stickers are sizzling, about 2 minutes.

TO MAKE THE DIPPING SAUCE, mix all of the ingredients in a small bowl. Serve the pot stickers with the sauce.

NOTE: Hot chili oil is sesame or vegetable oil flavored with hot chile peppers to make a spicy condiment. It is not used for cooking. It is available in Asian markets and many supermarkets.

Shrimp con Queso

Everyone loves *chile con queso*, but wait until you try it with shrimp! Our fondness for spicy foods has led to a proliferation of hot sauces on the shelves of gourmet shops and grocery stores and you may find some interesting Mexican types to add heat to your *queso*. The best way to keep it warm is in a mini crockpot or a fondue pot.

IN A MEDIUM NONSTICK SAUCEPAN, heat the oil over medium heat. Add the onion and jalapeño and cook, stirring often, until the onion is translucent, about 4 minutes. Add the garlic and cook until fragrant, about 1 minute. Add the tomatoes and cook, stirring often, until they give off their juices and they evaporate, about 5 minutes. (The mixture should look somewhat dry.) Add the milk and bring to a simmer.

IN A MEDIUM BOWL, toss the Monterey jack and cheddar with the cornstarch. Stir the cheese into the milk mixture, a handful at a time, stirring each batch until it melts before adding another. Stir in the shrimp. Season with the hot sauce. Transfer to a mini crockpot or fondue pot. Serve warm, with the tortilla chips for dipping.

1 tablespoon olive oil

1 medium onion, chopped

1 jalapeño, seeded and minced

2 garlic cloves, minced

1 can (16 ounces) peeled tomatoes in juice, drained and finely chopped

¾ cup milk

2 cups (8 ounces) shredded Monterey jack cheese

2 cups (8 ounces) shredded extra-sharp cheddar cheese

1 tablespoon cornstarch

1 pound medium shrimp, cooked, peeled, deveined, and finely chopped (see page 17)

Hot Mexican pepper sauce, to taste

Tortilla chips, for dipping

MAKES 6 TO 8 SERVINGS

2 tablespoons vegetable oil

4 cups thinly shredded napa cabbage

8 ounces ground pork

3 scallions, white and green parts, finely chopped

1 medium celery rib, finely chopped

8 ounces medium shrimp, peeled, deveined, and finely chopped

2 tablespoons finely chopped fresh cilantro

1 tablespoon soy sauce

1 tablespoon dry sherry

½ teaspoon salt

1½ teaspoons cornstarch

15 egg roll wrappers

Vegetable oil, for brushing

Hot Chinese mustard, for serving

Duck sauce, for serving

MAKES ABOUT 15 ROLLS

Baked Shrimp Spring Rolls

Crisp deep-fried spring rolls are great, but baking makes a nice change. Be sure that your filling is completely cooled and well drained, or the rolls will become soggy.

IN A LARGE (12-INCH) NONSTICK SKILLET, heat 1 tablespoon of the oil over medium-high heat. Add the cabbage and stir-fry until wilted and tender, about 3 minutes. (It may scorch slightly, but that will add flavor.) Transfer to a large colander and set aside.

ADD THE REMAINING 1 TABLESPOON OIL to the skillet and heat over medium-high heat. Add the pork, scallions, and celery and stir-fry until the pork loses its pink color, about 2 minutes. Add the shrimp, cilantro, soy sauce, sherry, and salt and stir-fry until the shrimp turns pink, about 1 minute. Transfer to the colander. Let stand, stirring occasionally, until cooled, about 30 minutes. Press firmly on the filling to remove excess moisture. Stir in the cornstarch.

PREHEAT THE OVEN TO 375° F. Brush a baking sheet with the vegetable oil.

PLACE AN EGG ROLL WRAPPER on a work surface, point up. Place about ¼ cup of the filling on the bottom third of the wrapper. Dab the bottom point with water. Fold in the side points and roll up to form a cylinder. Place the spring roll, seam side down, on the baking sheet. Repeat with the remaining filling and wrappers. Brush the spring rolls lightly with oil.

BAKE THE EGG ROLLS UNTIL LIGHTLY BROWNED, about 10 minutes. Turn and continue baking until golden brown, about 10 minutes more. Serve warm, with bowls of mustard and duck sauce to mix into a dipping sauce to taste.

Cilantro Shrimp Toasts

Shrimp toasts are one of life's great culinary indulgences. Fortunately, they can be fried a couple of hours ahead of serving time, though, like all fried foods, they are at their best when freshly prepared.

IN A FOOD PROCESSOR, PROCESS THE SHRIMP, egg white, fish sauce, sugar, salt, and red pepper until smooth. Add the shallots, cilantro, and garlic and pulse until combined. Transfer to a small bowl. Spread the shrimp paste on the baguette slices, mounding the paste slightly in the center.

PREHEAT THE OVEN TO 200° F. Place a cake rack over a baking sheet.

IN A LARGE, HEAVY SKILLET, melt enough vegetable shortening over medium-high heat to come halfway up the sides and heat to 360° F. Working in batches without crowding, deep-fry the toasts, shrimp side down, for 90 seconds, spooning the oil over the toasts. Turn and continue frying, spooning some of the oil over the toasts, until golden brown, about 1 minute. Transfer the toasts to the wire rack and keep warm in the oven while frying the remaining toasts. Serve immediately, with the sauce for dipping. (The toasts may be kept at room temperature for up to 1 hour and reheated in a 400° F. oven for about 7 minutes.)

NOTE: Asian fish sauce (*nam pla* or *nuoc mam*) and Indonesian fish sauce (*pastis*) are available in Asian markets, many supermarkets, or by mail order (see page 161). While pastis is milder, the three are interchangeable. A combination of equal amounts of soy sauce, Worcestershire sauce, and water may be substituted for the fish sauce.

1 pound medium shrimp, peeled and deveined

1 large egg white

1 tablespoon Asian fish sauce (see Note)

1 teaspoon sugar

½ teaspoon salt

¼ teaspoon crushed red pepper

2 tablespoons minced shallots

2 tablespoons finely chopped fresh cilantro, including stems

1 garlic clove, crushed through a press

24 baguette slices, cut on the diagonal ¼-inch thick

Vegetable shortening, for deep-frying

Sweet-and-Tangy Dipping Sauce (page 61)

MAKES ABOUT 48 TOASTS

SHRIMP SEVICHE

1½ pounds medium shrimp, peeled, deveined, and cut lengthwise in half

½ cup fresh lime juice

¼ cup extra virgin olive oil

½ medium red onion, thinly sliced

½ habanero chile pepper or 1 jalapeño pepper, seeded and thinly sliced

½ teaspoon salt

GRAPEFRUIT-AVOCADO SALSA

2 medium ruby grapefruits

1 ripe medium avocado

⅓ cup finely chopped red bell pepper

2 tablespoons finely chopped red onion

1 tablespoon fresh lime juice

½ fresh habanero chile pepper or 1 jalapeño pepper, seeded and thinly sliced

1 garlic clove, crushed through a press

¼ teaspoon salt

Chopped fresh cilantro, oregano, or mint, for garnish

MAKES 6 SERVINGS

Shrimp Seviche with Grapefruit-Avocado Salsa

Seviche—fish or shellfish marinated in citrus juice until "cooked" by the juice's acidity—must be made with the highest-quality ingredients, so be sure to buy the best shrimp you can from the most reliable source. This dish is prepared with the ultra-spicy habanero pepper; use it with a light hand.

TO MAKE THE SEVICHE, combine all of the ingredients in a medium bowl. Cover and refrigerate until the shrimps look opaque, at least 4 hours or up to 8 hours. Do not overmarinate. (If not serving immediately, drain, cover, and refrigerate for up to 1 day.)

TO MAKE THE SALSA, peel the grapefruits. Using a sharp knife and working over a bowl, cut in between the grapefruit membranes to release the fruit sections. Cut the grapefruit into ½-inch cubes. Place in a medium bowl.

CUT THE AVOCADO LENGTHWISE IN HALF and remove the pit. Make crosshatch cuts into the avocado flesh, reaching down to, but not cutting through, the peel. Using a large spoon, scoop out the avocado and add to the grapefruit. Add the bell pepper, onion, lime juice, habanero, garlic, and salt and mix gently. Cover and refrigerate just until chilled, at least 2 hours.

TO SERVE, PLACE 6 WIDE GLASSES IN THE FREEZER for 10 minutes to chill. Sort through the seviche, discarding the onion and chile slices and the garlic. Spoon equal portions of the salsa into the glasses. Top with equal portions of seviche and sprinkle with the cilantro. Serve chilled.

Scandinavian Vodka-Soused Shrimp

Long-marinated shrimp are a Scandinavian specialty. Serve this vodka-soaked version with slices of buttered pumpernickel bread.

1 large bunch (3 ounces) fresh dill

2 large lemons, sliced into ¼-inch rounds

2 teaspoons salt

1 teaspoon whole black peppercorns

2 pounds large shrimp

½ cup high-quality vodka

MAKES 6 TO 8 SERVINGS

THE DAY BEFORE SERVING, cut off the dill stems and set aside. Cover the dill fronds and refrigerate.

IN A LARGE POT, BRING 4 CUPS WATER, dill stems, lemons, salt, and peppercorns to a boil over high heat. Reduce the heat to medium and simmer for 10 minutes. Add the shrimp and cook until pink and firm, 2 to 3 minutes (the water does not have to return to the boil). Using a slotted spoon, transfer the shrimps to a large baking sheet to cool completely. Strain the cooking liquid into a medium bowl, reserving the solids.

PEEL AND DEVEIN THE SHRIMPS and arrange in a 9-inch square glass or ceramic baking dish. Scatter the dill stems, lemon slices, and a few peppercorns over the shrimp. Pour in the vodka and enough of the strained cooking liquid to cover the shrimp completely. Cover tightly with plastic wrap and refrigerate for at least 8 hours and up to 24 hours.

WHEN READY TO SERVE, finely chop the dill fronds. Drain the shrimp, arrange on a platter, and sprinkle with the dill. Serve chilled.

Pickled Picnic Shrimp

Serve these at a picnic (or any party, really) and watch them disappear.

IN A MEDIUM NONREACTIVE POT, bring the vinegar, allspice berries, dill seeds, mustard seeds, peppercorns, cloves, cinnamon, garlic, sugar, and salt to a boil over high heat. Reduce the heat to medium-low and simmer for 10 minutes. Increase the heat to high. Add the shrimp and cover. Cook until pink and firm, 2 to 3 minutes (the liquid does not have to return to a boil).

USING A SLOTTED SPOON, transfer the shrimps to a large baking sheet to cool completely. Strain the cooking liquid into a medium bowl. Peel and devein the shrimps. Layer the shrimps with the onion and lemon slices, parsley, and bay leaves in a 9-inch square glass or ceramic baking dish or a large glass jar. Gradually whisk the oil into the cooking liquid and pour over the shrimps. Cover tightly with plastic wrap and refrigerate for at least 8 hours and up to 36 hours.

TO SERVE, strain the shrimp and arrange on a platter. Serve chilled.

2 cups cider vinegar

1 teaspoon allspice berries

1 teaspoon dill seeds

1 teaspoon mustard seeds

1 teaspoon whole black peppercorns

6 whole cloves

1 cinnamon stick (3 inches)

2 garlic cloves, crushed under a knife

2 teaspoons sugar

1 teaspoon salt

2 pounds large shrimp

1 medium onion, sliced

1 lemon, thinly sliced

2 tablespoons chopped fresh parsley

4 bay leaves

1 cup olive oil

1 cup vegetable oil

MAKES 6 TO 8 SERVINGS

Potted Shrimp with Dill and Dijon Mustard

1 pound medium shrimp, peeled (shells reserved) and deveined

8 tablespoons (1 stick) unsalted butter

1 tablespoon fresh lemon juice

1 tablespoon Dijon mustard

1 garlic clove, crushed through a press

1 tablespoon chopped fresh dill

Assorted crackers, for serving

MAKES ABOUT 1½ CUPS

Potted shrimp is easy to make and nice to have on hand to slather onto crackers for serving with drinks. The extra step of sautéing the shells isn't superfluous—it adds flavor and color to the spread.

IN A LARGE (12-INCH) NONSTICK SKILLET, melt the butter over medium heat. Add the shrimp shells and sauté, stirring occasionally, until the butter is bubbling and the shells are bright pink, about 3 minutes. Transfer to a food processor and process until the shells are coarsely chopped. Strain through a fine wire sieve into a bowl. Rinse out the food processor.

POUR THE BUTTER BACK INTO THE SKILLET and heat over medium-high heat. Add the shrimp and cook, turning once, until pink and firm, 2 to 3 minutes.

TRANSFER THE SHRIMPS AND BUTTER into the food processor. Add the lemon juice, mustard, and garlic and process until smooth. Add the dill and pulse to combine. Transfer to a small crock or bowl. Cover tightly with plastic wrap and refrigerate to blend the flavors, at least 2 hours or up to 2 days. Remove the potted shrimp from the refrigerator 30 minutes before serving. Serve as a spread with the crackers.

Crostini with Shrimp, Capers, and Olives

Crostini start with slices of toasted bread. (The bread can also be cut thicker and grilled for bruschetta.) Either way, spread with this smooth shrimp puree, the toasts make mouthwatering appetizers, especially when served with a cool glass of white wine.

TO MAKE THE TOPPING, in a large (12-inch) nonstick skillet, heat 1 tablespoon of the oil over medium heat. Add the shrimp and cook, turning once, until pink and firm, 2 to 3 minutes. Transfer to a food processor. Add the anchovy fillets, garlic, oregano, and red pepper. With the machine running, gradually add the remaining oil, processing until the mixture is smooth. Add the capers and pulse to mix. Transfer to a small bowl. Cover tightly and refrigerate to blend the flavors, at least 2 hours or up to 24 hours.

POSITION RACKS in the top third and center of the oven and preheat to 400° F.

IN A LARGE BOWL, toss the bread slices while drizzling with the oil. Arrange on baking sheets. Bake, switching the position of the sheets from top to bottom halfway during baking to ensure even browning, until the crostini are golden brown, about 10 minutes. Cool completely. (The crostini can be prepared up to 1 day ahead and stored in a paper bag at room temperature.)

TO SERVE, SPREAD THE TOPPING on the crostini and garnish with the chopped olives. Serve immediately.

SHRIMP TOPPING

¾ cup extra virgin olive oil

1 pound medium shrimp, peeled and deveined

6 anchovy fillets packed in oil, drained and chopped

1 garlic clove, crushed through a press

½ teaspoon dried oregano

⅛ teaspoon crushed red pepper, or more to taste

2 tablespoons bottled capers, rinsed, chopped if large

36 baguette slices, cut on the diagonal ¼-inch thick

3 tablespoons extra virgin olive oil

½ cup pitted and chopped Mediterranean black olives, for garnish

MAKES 36 CROSTINI

½ cup mayonnaise

1 tablespoon fresh lime juice

1 teaspoon chili powder

1 garlic clove, crushed through a press

4 flour tortillas (8 inches)

¾ pound medium shrimp, cooked, peeled, deveined, and coarsely chopped (page 17)

1½ cups (6 ounces) shredded Monterey jack cheese

1 large red bell pepper, roasted (directions follow) and cut into thin strips

Wooden toothpicks (optional)

MAKES 6 TO 8 SERVINGS

Shrimp and Roasted Red Pepper Mini Wraps

Wrapped sandwiches are taking over lunch menus across the country. Refrigerated (to help them hold their shape) and cut into thick slices, they can make the transition from lunch entrée to appetizer.

IN A MEDIUM BOWL, mix the mayonnaise, lime juice, chili powder, and garlic.

HEAT A LARGE SKILLET over medium heat. Place 1 tortilla in the skillet and cook, turning once, until heated through and lightly dotted with brown spots, about 1 minute. Spread the tortilla with 2 tablespoons of the mayonnaise mixture. Sprinkle with one fourth of the shrimp, followed by one fourth of the cheese. Cover with one fourth of the red pepper strips, with all of the strips facing east to west. Starting from the bottom, roll up tightly into a cylinder. Repeat with the remaining tortillas and fillings. Serve immediately. Or, to serve as an appetizer, wrap each roll in plastic, and refrigerate for at least 1 hour and up to 6 hours. Unwrap and use a serrated knife to cut into 1-inch-thick slices. If necessary, spear each slice through its sides with a wooden toothpick to keep it from unraveling while eating. Serve chilled.

NOTE: To roast a red bell pepper, position a broiler rack about 6 inches from the source of heat and preheat the broiler. Roast the pepper, turning occasionally, until charred all over. Depending on the size of the pepper and the heat, it should take about 10 minutes. Using a sharp knife, remove the charred skin, ribs, stem, and seeds. Rinse under cold running water if necessary. The pepper can also be roasted by placing the pepper directly on the grid of a gas burner on high heat, or in an outdoor charcoal or gas grill.

New Orleans Shrimp and Artichoke Terrine

A Creole reworking of a classic shrimp terrine.

IN A MEDIUM BOWL, sprinkle the gelatin over the water and let stand until the gelatin absorbs the water, about 5 minutes. Stir in the boiling stock and stir until the gelatin is completely dissolved, about 1 minute.

IN ANOTHER MEDIUM BOWL, dissolve the tomato paste in the lemon juice. Whisk in the mayonnaise and mustard. Whisk in the dissolved gelatin. Place the bowl in a larger bowl or roasting pan filled with iced water. Let stand, stirring occasionally, until the mixture is chilled and partially set (about the consistency of egg white), 15 to 20 minutes. Fold in the shrimp, artichoke hearts, scallions, and capers.

IN A CHILLED MEDIUM BOWL, whip the cream just until stiff. Fold into the shrimp mixture. Fold in the salt and hot pepper sauce and taste for seasoning. The terrine should be highly seasoned, since it will be served chilled and cold temperatures dull flavors.

LIGHTLY OIL A 9 X 5-INCH GLASS LOAF PAN and line the bottom with wax paper. Transfer the terrine mixture to the pan and smooth the top. Cover tightly and refrigerate until chilled and set, at least 4 hours or overnight.

HEAT A THIN-BLADED KNIFE under hot running water. Run the knife around the edges of the terrine to release it from the sides of the pan. Hold a serving platter over the top of the pan and invert the terrine onto the platter. Remove the wax paper. Using a thin-bladed knife, cut the terrine into slices. Place the slices on plates and garnish with the chopped tomatoes. Serve chilled.

2 envelopes plain gelatin

½ cup cold water

1 cup Shrimp Stock (page 16), heated to boiling

1 tablespoon tomato paste

2 tablespoons fresh lemon juice

¾ cup mayonnaise

4 teaspoons Creole Mustard (see page 24)

1 pound medium shrimp, cooked, peeled, deveined, and coarsely chopped (page 17)

1 package (10 ounces) thawed frozen artichoke hearts, finely chopped

2 scallions, white and green parts, finely chopped

1 tablespoon bottled capers, rinsed, and chopped if large

¾ cup heavy cream

½ teaspoon salt, or more to taste

½ teaspoon hot red pepper sauce, or more to taste

6 ripe plum tomatoes, seeded and finely chopped, for garnish

MAKES 8 TO 12 SERVINGS

Shrimp in the Salad Bowl

Shrimp, Salami, and White Bean Salad on Radicchio
Grilled Shrimp Caesar Salad
Corn, Shrimp, and Feta Salad with Chili-Lime Vinaigrette
Curried Shrimp and Apple Salad in Pita Bread
Shrimp, Fennel, and Blood Orange Salad
Provençal Shrimp, Potato, and Green Bean Salads on Mesclun
Italian Shrimp Salad with Olives and Basil
Shrimp and Sea Shell Pasta Salad with
*   Sun-Dried Tomato Vinaigrette*
Creamy Potato Salad with Shrimp and Dill
Grandma Rodgers's Shrimp and Iceberg Slaw
Vietnamese Shrimp Salad in Rice Paper Wrappers
Wilted Spinach and Shrimp Salad

PROVENÇAL SHRIMP, POTATO, AND
GREEN BEAN SALADS ON MESCLUN

8 ounces (1 cup) dried white beans, such as cannellini, rinsed and sorted for stones

1 small onion, cut in half

½ teaspoon salt

1 pound medium shrimp, cooked, peeled, and deveined (page 17)

5 ounces salami, sliced ⅛ inch thick and cut into ¼-inch-thick strips

2 tablespoons chopped fresh sage or 2 teaspoons dried sage

2 medium heads radicchio, cored and cut into ¼-inch-thick shreds

DRESSING

¼ cup red wine vinegar, or more to taste

2 garlic cloves, crushed through a press

1 teaspoon salt, or more to taste

¼ teaspoon crushed red pepper, or more to taste

1 cup extra virgin olive oil

MAKES 6 MAIN-COURSE SERVINGS

Shrimp, Salami, and White Bean Salad on Radicchio

Creamy white beans, garlicky salami, pungent sage, sweet shrimp, and bitter radicchio harmonize into a Mediterranean-inspired first course. Like potato salads and pasta salads, bean salads have a tendency to soak up dressings, so always taste them before serving. Add more vinegar, oil, salt, and hot pepper as needed.

PLACE THE BEANS IN A LARGE BOWL and add enough cold water to cover by 2 inches. Let stand at room temperature for at least 4 hours or overnight.

DRAIN THE BEANS and place in a medium saucepan. Add enough cold water to cover by 2 inches and add the onion. Bring to a boil over high heat. Reduce the heat to medium-low and simmer until the beans are almost tender, 30 to 40 minutes. Add the salt and simmer until the beans are just tender, about 10 more minutes, depending on how dry the beans are. Remove from the heat and cool the beans in the cooking liquid until they are lukewarm. Drain, remove the onion, and transfer to a large bowl. Add the shrimp and salami.

TO MAKE THE DRESSING, in a medium bowl, whisk the vinegar, garlic, salt, and hot pepper. Gradually whisk in the oil. Pour 1 cup of the dressing over the shrimp and beans, add the sage, and toss well. Cover with plastic wrap and refrigerate until ready to serve.

REMOVE THE SALAD FROM THE REFRIGERATOR 30 minutes before serving. Taste and adjust the seasoning. Toss the radicchio with the remaining ¼ cup dressing. Divide the radicchio among 6 six plates and top with equal amounts of the salad. Serve immediately.

Grilled Shrimp Caesar Salad

Caesar salad's famous anchovy dressing enhances the flavor of grilled shrimp. The dressing is traditionally made with a coddled egg, but since many of today's cooks prefer to avoid undercooked eggs, I have omitted it. If the dressing is made in a blender, it will be almost as thick as the original. The dressing does double duty here, acting as a marinade for the shrimp.

TO MAKE THE DRESSING, combine all of the ingredients except the oil in a blender. With the machine running, gradually pour in the oil.

IN A GLASS OR CERAMIC BOWL, toss the shrimp with 3 tablespoons of the dressing. Cover and refrigerate for at least 30 minutes and up to 2 hours. Cover and refrigerate the remaining dressing.

MEANWHILE, BUILD A MEDIUM-HOT CHARCOAL FIRE in an outdoor grill or preheat a gas grill on high, then reduce the heat to medium. Lightly oil the grill. Grill the shrimps, covered, turning once, until pink and firm, 6 to 8 minutes.

IN A LARGE BOWL, TOSS THE LETTUCE with the remaining dressing. Divide among 4 large plates and top each serving with 4 shrimp and 2 toasted baguette slices. Using a vegetable peeler, shave curls of Parmesan over each serving. Serve immediately.

CAESAR DRESSING

- 3 tablespoons fresh lemon juice
- 2 teaspoons anchovy paste or drained and minced anchovy fillets in oil
- 2 garlic cloves, crushed through a press
- ¼ teaspoon salt
- ¼ teaspoon freshly ground pepper
- ¾ cup extra virgin olive oil

- 16 colossal shrimp (U/15), peeled and deveined
- 1 medium head romaine lettuce, torn into bite-size pieces, rinsed and dried
- 8 slices French or Italian baguette, toasted
- 1 chunk (2-ounce) Parmesan cheese

MAKES 4 MAIN-COURSE SERVINGS

Corn, Shrimp, and Feta Salad with Chili-Lime Vinaigrette

Here's a colorful salad that will add zest to any backyard cookout. Grilling the corn is easy, especially on a gas grill—soaking and husking the corn beforehand is totally unnecessary.

TO MAKE THE DRESSING, in a medium bowl, whisk the lime juice, chili powder, oregano, garlic, salt, and pepper. Gradually whisk in the oil.

IN A MEDIUM GLASS OR CERAMIC BOWL, toss the shrimp with 3 tablespoons of the dressing. Cover and refrigerate for at least 30 minutes and up to 2 hours. Cover and refrigerate the remaining dressing.

MEANWHILE, BUILD A HOT CHARCOAL FIRE in an outdoor grill or preheat a gas grill on high. Lightly oil the grill. Place the shrimps and corn on the grill and cover. Grill the shrimps, turning once, until pink and firm, about 5 minutes. Cover and refrigerate the shrimp until ready to use. Continue to grill the corn, turning occasionally, until the husks are scorched on all sides, about 12 minutes more.

COOL THE CORN UNTIL EASY TO HANDLE. Remove the husks and silk. Using a sharp knife, cut the end of an ear of corn. Stand the corn on end and hold firmly. Use the knife to cut down the cob, cutting away the kernels. Repeat with the remaining ears of corn. You should have 2 cups of corn.

CUT EACH SHRIMP LENGTHWISE IN HALF. In a large serving bowl, toss the shrimps, corn, tomatoes, scallions, and jalapeño with the remaining vinaigrette. Cover and refrigerate until chilled, about 2 hours. Taste and adjust the seasoning with lime juice, salt, and pepper as needed. Sprinkle with the feta cheese and serve.

CHILI-LIME VINAIGRETTE

- 3 tablespoons fresh lime juice, or more to taste
- 1 tablespoon chili powder
- 2 teaspoons dried oregano
- 1 garlic clove, crushed through a press
- ½ teaspoon salt, or more to taste
- ¼ teaspoon freshly ground pepper, or more to taste
- ⅔ cup extra virgin olive oil

- 1 pound large shrimp, peeled and deveined
- 4 ears corn, with husks and silks
- 3 ripe plum tomatoes, seeded and cut into ½-inch cubes
- 2 scallions, white and green parts, trimmed and chopped
- 1 jalapeño, seeded and minced
- 3 ounces feta cheese, crumbled

MAKES 6 TO 8 SIDE-DISH SERVINGS

Nonstick vegetable oil spray

1 pound medium shrimp, peeled, deveined, and coarsely chopped

2 teaspoons Madras curry powder (see Note)

⅓ cup mayonnaise

3 tablespoons plain lowfat yogurt

¼ teaspoon salt

⅛ teaspoon freshly ground pepper

1 Golden Delicious apple, unpeeled, cored and cut into ½-inch cubes

1 small celery rib with leaves, minced

1 bunch (6 ounces) watercress, tough stems removed

4 pita breads, trimmed 2 inches from the top and opened to make pockets

MAKES 4 SANDWICHES

Curried Shrimp and Apple Salad in Pita Bread

This aromatic salad is a fine lunchtime entrée served on a bed of watercress, but I like it even more tucked into pita bread as a sandwich. This version is especially aromatic—heating the curry powder releases its full flavor potential by releasing the oils in the spices.

SPRAY A LARGE NONSTICK SKILLET with vegetable oil and heat over medium heat. Add the shrimp and cook until barely opaque, stirring occasionally, about 1½ minutes. Sprinkle with the curry powder and cook, stirring almost constantly, until the shrimps are pink and firm, about 1 minute, adjusting the heat, if needed, to keep the curry powder from scorching. Transfer to a medium bowl and cool completely.

ADD THE MAYONNAISE, YOGURT, SALT, and pepper and mix. Stir in the apple and celery. Cover with plastic wrap and refrigerate until chilled, about 1 hour.

SPOON EQUAL AMOUNTS OF THE SALAD into the pita breads, and tuck in the watercress leaves. Serve immediately.

NOTE: Madras curry powder is available in supermarkets in a familiar yellow can. It is a consistent, mildly hot blend of spices. Other curry powders (especially proprietary blends from spice stores) vary in heat intensity, so use them to taste.

Shrimp, Fennel, and Blood Orange Salad

Blood oranges used to be a rarity imported from Europe, but California-grown varieties have been making them a familiar winter sight in supermarket produce departments. This salad combines them with another winter favorite, fennel, creating an excellent main-course salad.

TO MAKE THE VINAIGRETTE, in a medium bowl, whisk the sherry vinegar, mustard, zest, salt, and pepper. Gradually whisk in the oil, then the parsley. Set aside.

IN A LARGE BOWL, COMBINE THE SHRIMP, fennel, and orange sections. Add the vinaigrette and toss well. Cover and refrigerate until ready to serve, up to 2 hours.

ARRANGE THE LETTUCE LEAVES ON 4 DINNER PLATES. Using a slotted spoon, place equal portions of the salad in the center of each plate. Drizzle the dressing left in the bowl over the lettuce and serve immediately. Sprinkle each serving with the chopped fennel fronds, if desired.

NOTE: If the fennel bulb is topped with feathery green fronds, trim them off, chop coarsely, and reserve about 2 tablespoons for the garnish. Trim away the stalks from the top of the bulb. Remove and discard the first thick layer of the fennel, which is usually bruised. Cut the bulb in half lengthwise. Cut away the hard solid core from each half. Place the fennel cut side down and cut crosswise into thin slices. Use the fennel immediately, or it may discolor.

ORANGE VINAIGRETTE

2 tablespoons sherry vinegar

2 teaspoons grainy prepared mustard, such as Moutarde de Meaux

Grated zest of 1 orange

½ teaspoon salt

¼ teaspoon freshly ground pepper

⅔ cup extra virgin olive oil

2 tablespoons chopped fresh parsley

1 pound medium shrimp, cooked, peeled, and deveined (page 17)

1 medium (1 pound) bulb fennel, trimmed (see Note) and cut into ⅛-inch-thick half moons

3 blood oranges or 2 navel oranges, peeled and cut between membranes into individual segments

1 head Bibb lettuce, separated into leaves, rinsed, and dried

Chopped fennel fronts, for garnish (optional)

MAKES 4 MAIN-COURSE SERVINGS

Provençal Shrimp, Potato, and Green Bean Salads on Mesclun

My version of salade niçoise features three little salads on a bed of mesclun, the classic provençal salad greens mixture that used to be found only in rural French farmer's markets but now shows up in mainstream supermarkets. Our mass-market mesclun often includes too many bitter, peppery greens, which can be mellowed with the addition of mellower, sweeter lettuces, such as red leaf or Bibb.

TO MAKE THE VINAIGRETTE, in a medium bowl, whisk the vinegar, mustard, salt, and pepper. Gradually whisk in the oil. Stir in the shallots. Set aside.

BRING A LARGE POT OF LIGHTLY SALTED WATER TO A BOIL over high heat. Add the green beans and cook until crisp-tender, 2 to 3 minutes for regular green beans, about 1½ minutes for haricots verts. Using a slotted skimmer, transfer the green beans to a colander. Rinse under cold water and drain. Transfer to a bowl, cover, and refrigerate until ready to serve.

IN THE SAME POT OF BOILING WATER, cook the shrimp until pink and firm, 2 to 3 minutes (the water does not have to return to a boil). Using a slotted skimmer, transfer the shrimps to a bowl. Cool until easy to handle, then peel and devein. Place the shrimps in a medium bowl. Add the cherry tomatoes, 1 tablespoon of the parsley, and ¼ cup of the vinaigrette. Toss well and season with salt and pepper. Cover and refrigerate until well chilled, at least 1 hour and up to 4 hours.

IN THE SAME POT OF BOILING WATER, cook the potatoes until tender, 20 to 30 minutes depending on the size of the potatoes. Drain and rinse under cold water until cool enough to handle. Slice into ¼-inch-thick rounds. Place in a medium bowl and toss with ¼ cup of the vinaigrette and 1 tablespoon of the parsley. Season with salt and pepper. Cover and refrigerate until well chilled, at least 1 hour and up to 4 hours.

JUST BEFORE SERVING, TOSS THE GREEN BEANS with 2 tablespoons of the vinaigrette and the remaining parsley. Season with salt and pepper.

IN A LARGE BOWL, TOSS THE MESCLUN with the remaining dressing. Place equal amounts of mesclun on 4 dinner plates. Place one fourth of the 3 salads on each plate. Serve immediately.

Italian Shrimp Salad
with Olives and Basil

2 medium lemons, sliced

2½ pounds medium shrimp

1 cup coarsely chopped pitted
Mediterranean black olives

3 tablespoons fresh lemon juice

½ teaspoon salt

¼ teaspoon crushed red pepper

½ cup extra virgin olive oil

3 tablespoons chopped fresh basil

Lemon wedges, for serving

**MAKES 4 TO 6 MAIN-COURSE
SERVINGS**

Simple seafood salads like this grace the antipasto
tables of restaurants throughout Italy. For the best
flavor, serve it at cool room temperature, not ice cold.

IN A MEDIUM SAUCEPAN, bring 2 quarts lightly salted water and the
lemon slices to a boil over high heat. Add the shrimp and cook until
pink and firm, 2 to 3 minutes. (The water does not have to return to a
boil.) Drain and rinse under cold water until easy to handle. Peel and
devein the shrimps. Place in a medium bowl and add the olives.

IN A SMALL BOWL, WHISK THE LEMON JUICE, salt, and red pepper.
Gradually whisk in the oil. Pour over the shrimp and toss well. Cover
and refrigerate until ready to serve, up to 4 hours.

REMOVE FROM THE REFRIGERATOR 30 MINUTES BEFORE SERVING. Add
the basil and toss. Serve with the lemon wedges on the side for squeezing
over each serving.

Shrimp and Sea Shell Pasta Salad with Sun-Dried Tomato Vinaigrette

Sun-dried tomatoes, blended with vinegar and oil, make a flavorful, thick dressing. Like all pasta salads, be sure to season this one before serving, as the pasta will soak up the vinaigrette and flatten the flavor as it stands.

TO MAKE THE VINAIGRETTE, in a blender, combine the sun-dried tomatoes, vinegar, oregano, garlic, salt, and pepper. With the machine running, gradually add the oil. Set the vinaigrette aside.

BRING A LARGE POT OF LIGHTLY SALTED WATER to a boil over high heat. Add the shrimp and cook until pink and firm, 2 to 3 minutes. (The water does not have to return to a boil.) Using a slotted skimmer, transfer the shrimps to a colander and rinse under cold water until easy to handle. Peel and devein the shrimps. Cut each shrimp lengthwise in half. Place in a large bowl.

IN THE SAME POT OF BOILING WATER, cook the pasta until tender according to the package instructions. Drain and rinse under cold water until cool. Drain well. Transfer to the bowl of shrimp.

ADD THE CELERY, SCALLIONS, OLIVES, AND VINAIGRETTE and toss well. Cover and refrigerate until chilled, at least 2 hours or up to overnight. Stir in the basil. Taste and add more vinegar, salt, and red pepper as needed. Serve immediately.

NOTE: Replace some of the olive oil with oil from the tomatoes, if you wish.

SUN-DRIED TOMATO VINAIGRETTE

½ cup drained and chopped sun-dried tomatoes packed in olive oil

2 tablespoons red wine vinegar, or more to taste

½ teaspoon dried oregano

1 garlic clove, crushed through a press

¼ teaspoon salt, or more to taste

½ teaspoon crushed red pepper, or more to taste

½ cup extra virgin olive oil (see Note)

1 pound medium shrimp

8 ounces medium sea shell pasta

3 medium celery ribs, finely chopped

3 scallions, white and green parts, finely chopped

½ cup chopped pitted Mediterranean green olives

2 tablespoons chopped fresh basil

MAKES 4 TO 6 MAIN-COURSE SERVINGS

Creamy Potato Salad
with Shrimp and Dill

This is a potato salad for grown-ups. I created it as a luxurious side dish for grilled salmon, but now I serve it as a summer lunch entrée as well.

1 pound medium shrimp, unpeeled

2 pounds small new potatoes, scrubbed, or medium red potatoes, scrubbed and cut into 1-inch cubes

1 tablespoon white wine vinegar, or more to taste

½ cup mayonnaise

1 tablespoon Dijon mustard

½ cup sour cream

4 anchovy fillets packed in oil, drained and mashed to a paste, or 2 teaspoons anchovy paste

½ teaspoon salt, or more to taste

¼ teaspoon freshly ground pepper, or more to taste

1 cup chopped scallions, green and white parts

2 tablespoons chopped fresh dill

2 tablespoons bottled capers, rinsed and coarsely chopped if large

MAKES 6 MAIN-COURSE OR 8 SIDE-DISH SERVINGS

BRING A LARGE POT OF LIGHTLY SALTED WATER to a boil over high heat. Add the shrimp and cook until pink and firm, 2 to 3 minutes. (The water does not have to return to a boil.) Using a large skimmer, transfer the shrimps to a colander, keeping the water in the pot at a boil. Rinse the shrimps under cold running water until easy to handle, then peel and devein. Place in a bowl, cover, and refrigerate until ready to use.

ADD THE POTATOES TO THE BOILING WATER and reduce the heat to medium. Simmer until the potatoes are just tender when pierced with the tip of a knife, about 20 minutes. Drain the potatoes and place in a medium serving bowl. Sprinkle the potatoes with the vinegar. Let the potatoes cool to room temperature.

IN A SMALL BOWL, MIX THE MAYONNAISE, sour cream, mustard, anchovies, salt, and pepper. Add the shrimps, scallions, dill, and capers to the potatoes and mix with the mayonnaise dressing. Cover and refrigerate until well chilled, at least 2 hours or up to 8 hours. Just before serving, taste and add more salt, pepper, and vinegar, if needed. Serve chilled.

Grandma Rodgers's Shrimp and Iceberg Slaw

Iceberg lettuce has sadly become the Danish furniture of the salad bowl—once revered, now often reviled. Many cooks (like me) never stopped loving the crisp crunch of chilled iceberg. This recipe from my grandmother was featured at many a backyard barbecue in my childhood. If you find homegrown iceberg lettuce from a roadside farmstand or farmer's market, you are in for a real treat.

IN A MEDIUM BOWL, whisk the mayonnaise, vinegar, onion, celery seeds, salt, and pepper. Add the shrimp, lettuce, and tomatoes, and toss well. Serve immediately. (The salad can be prepared up to 2 hours ahead, covered, and refrigerated. It will wilt slightly, but that is the way Grandma Rodgers served it.)

¾ cup mayonnaise, cold

2 tablespoons sherry or cider vinegar

1 tablespoon grated onion (use a small onion grated on the large holes of a cheese grater)

½ teaspoon celery seeds

½ teaspoon salt

¼ teaspoon freshly ground pepper

1 pound medium shrimp, cooked, peeled and deveined (page 17), or ready-cooked tiny pink shrimp, well chilled

1 medium head iceberg lettuce, cored and cut into ¼-inch-wide shreds, well chilled

4 ripe plum tomatoes, seeded and cut into ½-inch dice

MAKES 6 TO 8 SIDE-DISH SERVINGS

Vietnamese Shrimp Salad in Rice Paper Wrappers

The first time I tried this, fifteen years ago, I thought, "What is this salad wrapped in?" The mystery wrapper turned out to be a rice-paper round. They still aren't supermarket fare, but they can be easily found in Southeast Asian food stores. If you can't find them, enjoy the salad without the wrapping, sprinkled with chopped peanuts.

IN A MEDIUM BOWL, mix the lime juice, fish sauce, and chili sauce. Add the shrimps, scallion, carrot, mint, and cilantro and toss well. Cover and refrigerate for up to 2 hours.

FILL A SHALLOW DISH WITH WARM WATER. Place a clean kitchen towel next to the dish. Submerge the rice-paper rounds one at a time in the water and let stand just until pliable, about 15 seconds, depending on the age and dryness of the round. Lift out the round and place it on the towel (it will soften more as it stands).

PLACE 1/4 OF THE SALAD on the bottom third of the round. Fold up the bottom edge to cover the salad, tuck in the 2 sides, and roll up the wrapper to make a thick cylinder. Repeat with the remaining rounds and salad. (The rolls can be prepared up to 2 hours ahead, covered loosely with plastic wrap, and refrigerated.)

TO MAKE THE DIPPING SAUCE, combine the ingredients in a small bowl, stirring to dissolve the sugar. (The dipping sauce can be prepared up to 4 days ahead, covered, and refrigerated.)

(CONTINUED)

1 tablespoon fresh lime juice

1 tablespoon Asian fish sauce (see page 37)

½ teaspoon Vietnamese chili garlic sauce (see Note)

1 pound medium shrimp, cooked, peeled, deveined, and cut lengthwise in half (page 17)

1 scallion, white and green parts, minced

1 medium carrot, cut into very fine julienne

2 tablespoons chopped fresh mint

2 tablespoons chopped fresh cilantro

4 rice paper rounds (8 inches)

SWEET-AND-TANGY DIPPING SAUCE

¼ cup Asian fish sauce (see page 37)

¼ cup fresh lime juice

1 tablespoon light brown sugar

2 garlic cloves, minced

1 teaspoon crushed red pepper

MAKES 4 FIRST-COURSE SERVINGS

TO SERVE, CUT EACH ROLL CROSSWISE on a sharp diagonal. Divide the dipping sauce among 4 small bowls. Serve the rolls with the sauce, for dipping.

NOTE: Vietnamese chili sauce is a fire engine–red puree of serrano chiles, garlic, and vinegar. It is available at Asian grocers. Hot red pepper sauce, such as Tabasco, is an acceptable substitute, but add 1 small garlic clove, crushed through a press.

Wilted Spinach and Shrimp Salad

Wilted spinach salad often has bacon, but this lighter version stars shrimp. Save this recipe for when you have young, tender spinach with delicate stems—the tough-stemmed, cellophane-packaged supermarket kind just isn't as good.

IN A LARGE (12-INCH) SKILLET, heat 1 tablespoon of the oil over medium heat. Add the shrimps and cook, turning once, until pink and firm, 2 to 3 minutes. Using a slotted spoon, transfer to a plate. Cover with foil to keep warm.

ADD 2 TABLESPOONS OF OIL TO THE SKILLET and return to medium heat. Add the shallots and garlic and cook, stirring often, until softened, about 2 minutes. Add the vinegar, salt, and pepper and bring to a simmer. Briskly stir in the remaining oil and boil for 30 seconds.

PLACE THE SPINACH IN A LARGE BOWL. Add the hot vinaigrette and toss until the spinach wilts and is well coated. Divide the salad among 4 plates and top with the shrimps. Serve immediately.

¾ cup extra virgin olive oil

1 pound large shrimp, peeled and deveined

¼ cup minced shallots

2 garlic cloves, minced

¼ cup red wine vinegar

½ teaspoon salt

¼ teaspoon freshly ground pepper

1½ pounds tender fresh spinach, tough stems discarded, and well rinsed

MAKES 4 FIRST-COURSE SERVINGS

Shrimp from a Pot

Shrimp and Asparagus in Coriander Broth
Shrimp and Fennel Bisque
Chipotle Shrimp and Corn Chowder
Chinese Creamy Corn Soup with Shrimp
Shrimp Gazpacho
Shrimp and Okra Gumbo
Mandarin Hot-and-Sour Soup
Shrimp, Ramen, and Sugar Snap Pea Soup
Southeast Asian Shrimp Soup with Lemongrass and Chiles
Shrimp and Spinach Won Ton Soup
Beer and Spice Shrimp with Bumpy Mayonnaise
Low Country Shrimp, Sausage, and Corn Boil
Spicy Steamed Shrimp with Chesapeake Bay Spices

**SHRIMP AND ASPARAGUS
IN CORIANDER BROTH**

¾ pound thin asparagus spears, woody stems discarded and cut into ½-inch lengths

1 tablespoon unsalted butter

1 cup thinly sliced leeks, white parts only, separated into rounds and well rinsed

½ cup dry white wine

4 cups Shrimp Stock with Coriander (page 16)

½ teaspoon salt

⅛ teaspoon freshly ground white pepper

1 pound medium shrimp, peeled (use the shells in the stock), deveined, and cut lengthwise in halves

MAKES 4 SERVINGS

Shrimp and Asparagus in Coriander Broth

When you need a light first course to open a special meal, try this simple but elegant soup. Be sure to rinse the shrimps well under cold water before adding to the broth—this step removes any surface proteins that would cloud the soup.

BRING A MEDIUM SAUCEPAN of lightly salted water to a boil over high heat. Add the asparagus and cook until crisp-tender, about 3 minutes. Drain, rinse under cold water, and drain again. Set aside.

IN A MEDIUM SAUCEPAN, MELT THE BUTTER over medium heat. Add the leeks and cover. Cook, stirring occasionally, until the leeks are softened, about 5 minutes. Add the wine and bring to a boil. Add the stock, salt, and pepper and return to a boil. Reduce the heat to low, cover partially, and simmer for 10 minutes.

RINSE THE SHRIMP under cold running water.

STIR THE SHRIMPS AND ASPARAGUS into the broth and cook until the shrimps are pink and firm, about 3 minutes (the broth does not have to return to a boil). Serve immediately.

Shrimp and Fennel Bisque

Fennel's mild anise flavor is a perfect match for shrimp. This bisque is a luxurious way to open a holiday meal.

IN A MEDIUM SAUCEPAN, bring the shrimp shells and broth to a simmer over high heat. Reduce the heat to low and simmer for 30 minutes. Strain the stock into a bowl, discarding the shells. Set aside.

IN A LARGE DUTCH OVEN OR FLAMEPROOF CASSEROLE, heat the butter over medium-low heat. Add the fennel and shallots and cover. Cook until the fennel softens, about 10 minutes. Sprinkle with the flour and stir for 1 minute. Gradually stir in the broth. Stir in the vermouth and tomato paste. Bring to a simmer over high heat, stirring to dissolve the tomato paste. Return the heat to medium-low and simmer, uncovered, until the fennel is very tender, about 10 minutes. Add the shrimp and cook until pink and firm, about 3 minutes.

POUR THE MIXTURE INTO A WIRE SIEVE set over a bowl. Transfer the solids with about 2 cups of the liquid to a blender and process until smooth. Return the puree and the cooking liquid in the bowl to the saucepan. Add the heavy cream, and liqueur, if desired. Bring just to a simmer over medium heat. Season with the salt and pepper. Serve hot, garnishing each serving with chopped fennel fronds.

8 ounces medium shrimp, peeled (use the shells in the broth) and deveined

4 cups chicken broth, preferably home-made, or low-sodium canned broth

2 tablespoons unsalted butter

2 cups chopped (¼-inch dice) fennel bulb (see page 53)

⅓ cup finely chopped shallots

2 tablespoons all-purpose flour

⅓ cup dry vermouth

1 tablespoon tomato paste

½ cup heavy cream

2 teaspoons anise-flavor liqueur, such as Pernod (optional)

¼ teaspoon salt

¼ teaspoon freshly ground white pepper

Chopped fennel fronds, for garnish

MAKES 6 SERVINGS

6 ounces bacon, coarsely chopped

1 medium onion, chopped

1 medium celery rib with leaves, chopped

1 small red bell pepper, seeded and chopped

2 large garlic cloves, minced

2 tablespoons all-purpose flour

4 cups Shrimp Stock (page 16)

8 ounces medium shrimp, peeled (use the shells in the stock), deveined, and coarsely chopped

1 cup fresh or thawed frozen corn kernels

¾ cup heavy cream

1 teaspoon minced canned chipotle chile pepper plus 1 teaspoon of adobo sauce

½ teaspoon salt

Chopped cilantro leaves, for garnish

MAKES 6 TO 8 SERVINGS

Chipotle Shrimp and Corn Chowder

Chipotle chiles en adobo are smoked jalapeños in a thick, brick-red sauce (do not confuse them with dried chipotles). They are available in Mexican markets and many supermarkets. They give this creamy chowder a smoky spiciness. A little of the incendiary chipotle chile and its sauce goes a long way. Be careful when handling them or protect your hands with plastic gloves.

IN A LARGE DUTCH OVEN OR FLAMEPROOF CASSEROLE, cook the bacon over medium heat until crisp, about 4 minutes. Using a slotted spoon, transfer the bacon to a paper towel–lined plate. Set aside. Pour off all but 2 tablespoons of the bacon fat.

ADD THE ONION, CELERY, BELL PEPPER, AND GARLIC. Cook, stirring often, until the vegetables soften, about 5 minutes. Sprinkle with the flour and stir for 30 seconds. Gradually stir in the stock and bring to a simmer. Reduce the heat to medium-low and simmer for about 20 minutes.

ADD THE SHRIMP, CORN, CREAM, CHILE AND ITS SAUCE, and the reserved bacon. Cook just until the shrimps turn pink and firm, 2 to 3 minutes (the soup does not have to return to a boil). Season with the salt. Serve in warmed soup bowls, sprinkling each serving with the chopped cilantro.

Chinese Creamy Corn Soup with Shrimp

There are countless recipes for this soup, and they all use canned creamed corn and not fresh corn puree. There's no use fighting City Hall here—this soup makes a great quick supper.

IN A LARGE DUTCH OVEN OR FLAMEPROOF CASSEROLE, heat the oil over medium heat. Add the scallions, bell pepper, and ginger. Cook, stirring often, until the pepper is softened, about 3 minutes. Stir in the stock and creamed corn and bring to a simmer. Reduce the heat to low and simmer for 10 minutes.

IN A SMALL BOWL, MIX THE SOY SAUCE AND SHERRY. Add the cornstarch and stir until dissolved. Stir into the soup and simmer until slightly thickened, about 1 minute. Add the shrimp and cook until pink and firm, 2 to 3 minutes (the soup does not have to return to a boil). Serve hot.

2 tablespoons vegetable oil

2 scallions, white and green parts, chopped

1 medium red bell pepper, seeded and chopped

2 teaspoons minced fresh ginger

3 cups Asian Shrimp Stock (page 16)

2 cans (14¾ ounces each) creamed corn

2 tablespoons soy sauce

2 tablespoons dry sherry

1 tablespoon cornstarch

1 pound medium shrimp, peeled (use the shells in the stock) and deveined

MAKES 4 TO 6 SERVINGS

Shrimp Gazpacho

1 pound ripe tomatoes, seeded and cut into ½-inch dice

1 large cucumber, peeled, seeded, and cut into ½-inch dice

1 medium red bell pepper, seeded and cut into ½-inch dice

⅓ cup chopped red onion

2 garlic cloves, crushed through a press

2 cups canned tomato-clam juice, such as Clamato

2 tablespoons fresh lemon juice

¼ teaspoon salt

Hot red pepper sauce, to taste

1 pound medium shrimp, cooked, peeled, deveined, and coarsely chopped (see page 17)

Croutons, for garnish

MAKES 4 TO 6 SERVINGS

Summer is gazpacho time. Shrimp adds sustenance to this version, making it one of my favorite summer supper dishes. One word of advice: chop the vegetables by hand, not in a food processor, or they will give off too much juice and water down the soup.

IN A LARGE BOWL, COMBINE ALL OF THE INGREDIENTS except the shrimp and croutons. Cover and refrigerate until well chilled, at least 4 hours or overnight.

STIR IN THE SHRIMP. Serve topped with croutons.

Shrimp and Okra Gumbo

Gumbo is the soul of Cajun cooking. Skillet-toasted flour gives old-fashioned flavor with much less trouble (and less fat) than the traditional roux.

HEAT A LARGE SKILLET OVER MEDIUM-HIGH HEAT until hot, about 2 minutes. Add the flour and stir constantly, shaking the pan often, until the flour turns dark beige, about 5 minutes. Immediately transfer the browned flour to a plate. Set aside.

IN A LARGE DUTCH OVEN OR FLAMEPROOF CASSEROLE, heat the oil over medium heat. Add the sausage and cook, stirring often, until browned, about 5 minutes. Using a slotted spoon, transfer the sausage to a plate, leaving the oil in the pot. Set aside.

ADD THE ONION, CELERY, BELL PEPPER, AND GARLIC to the pot. Cook, stirring often, until the vegetables soften, about 5 minutes. Stir in the browned flour and Cajun Seasoning and stir until the vegetables are completely coated with flour. Gradually stir in the stock. Add the reserved sausage, the tomatoes with their juices, salt, and bay leaf. Bring to a simmer and reduce the heat to low. Simmer, stirring often to avoid scorching, for 20 minutes. Add the okra and simmer until tender, about 10 minutes. Stir in the shrimp, corn, and Worcestershire, and cook until the shrimps are pink and firm, about 3 minutes (the soup does not have to return to a boil). Season with hot pepper sauce. To serve, spoon the rice into individual bowls, then add the gumbo.

Cajun Seasoning

Mix 2 tablespoons sweet Hungarian paprika, 1 teaspoon each dried basil and dried thyme, ½ teaspoon each freshly ground pepper, garlic powder, and onion powder, and ¼ teaspoon cayenne. (Store, tightly covered, in a cool dry place.)

½ cup all-purpose flour

2 tablespoons vegetable oil

8 ounces spicy smoked sausage, such as andouille or kielbasa, cut into ½-inch cubes

1 large onion, chopped

2 large celery ribs, chopped

1 medium red bell pepper, seeded and chopped

3 large garlic cloves, minced

1 tablespoon Cajun Seasoning (recipe follows)

5 cups Shrimp Stock (page 16)

1 can (16 ounces) peeled plum tomatoes in juice, juices reserved, chopped

¾ teaspoon salt

1 bay leaf

8 ounces fresh okra, trimmed, and cut into ¼-inch-thick rounds, or 1 box (10 ounces) frozen cut okra

1 pound medium shrimp, peeled (use the shells in the stock) and deveined

1½ cups fresh or thawed frozen corn kernels

1 tablespoon Worcestershire sauce

Hot red pepper sauce, to taste

Hot cooked rice, for serving

MAKES AT LEAST 8 SERVINGS

8 dried black (shiitake) mushrooms (see Note)

3 tablespoons soy sauce

2 tablespoons plus 1 teaspoon rice vinegar

1 teaspoon hot chili oil (see page 34)

½ teaspoon salt

¼ teaspoon freshly ground pepper

2 tablespoons cornstarch

4 cups Asian Shrimp Stock (page 16)

1 can (8 ounces) sliced bamboo shoots, rinsed and cut into ¼-inch-wide strips

1 pound medium shrimp, peeled (use the shells in the stock) and deveined

6 ounces firm tofu, cut into ½-inch cubes

2 scallions, white and green parts, chopped

1 large egg, beaten

MAKES 4 TO 6 SERVINGS

Mandarin Hot-and-Sour Soup

Classic hot-and-sour soup is packed with all kinds of Chinese flora, like tiger lily buds and wood's ear mushrooms. This streamlined version uses more easily available ingredients, but the result is still delicious.

IN A SMALL BOWL, SOAK THE MUSHROOMS in 2 cups hot tap water until softened, 20 to 30 minutes. Lift out the mushrooms, cut off and discard the tough stems, and slice the caps into ¼-inch-thick strips. Set aside. Strain the liquid through a paper towel–lined sieve and reserve 1 cup of the soaking liquid.

IN A SMALL BOWL, MIX THE SOY SAUCE, vinegar, hot chili oil, salt, and pepper. Add the cornstarch and stir to dissolve. Set aside.

IN A LARGE DUTCH OVEN OR FLAMEPROOF CASSEROLE, bring the stock and the mushroom soaking liquid to a boil over high heat. Add the mushrooms and bamboo shoots and reduce the heat to medium to keep the soup at a brisk simmer. Stir in the shrimp, tofu, and scallions. Stir in the cornstarch mixture and cook until thickened, about 30 seconds. Stirring constantly, add the egg to the soup (it will form threads). Cook until the egg threads are set and the shrimps are pink and firm, about 1 minute. Serve hot.

NOTE: Dried black mushrooms can also be labeled dried Oriental mushrooms, or by their Japanese name, shiitake mushrooms. Asian markets sell them in a variety of sizes and qualities—get the best you can afford. Dried black mushrooms are also available in many supermarkets.

Shrimp, Ramen, and Sugar Snap Pea Soup

Instant ramen noodles are a great way to cook up a fast meal, but the seasoning packets in the bag aren't so wonderful. Why not make an easy, delicious broth from shrimp shells? It only takes an extra few minutes, and what a difference!

IN A MEDIUM SAUCEPAN, bring 4 cups of water, the shrimp shells, sherry, soy sauce, sugar, ginger, garlic, and peppercorns to a simmer over high heat. Reduce the heat to medium-low and simmer for 5 minutes. Strain in a wire sieve set over a bowl, pressing hard on the shells to extract all the flavor. Discard the solids in the sieve.

RETURN THE STRAINED BROTH TO THE SAUCEPAN and bring to a boil over high heat. Add the shrimp and cook for 1 minute. Add the peas and cook until the shrimps are pink and firm and the peas are bright green, 1 to 2 minutes more. Using a large skimmer or slotted spoon, transfer the shrimps and peas to 2 or 3 soup bowls and set aside.

RETURN THE BROTH TO A FULL BOIL over high heat. Add the noodles and boil, breaking up the noodles with a spoon, until tender, about 3 minutes. Stir in the scallion, carrots, and sesame oil. Ladle into the soup bowls and serve, with hot chili oil and soy sauce passed at the table.

8 ounces medium shrimp, peeled (use the shells in the stock) and deveined

2 tablespoons dry sherry

1 tablespoon soy sauce, plus more for serving

¼ teaspoon sugar

2 quarter-size slices fresh ginger

2 garlic cloves, crushed

8 whole black peppercorns

2 packages (3 ounces each) ramen noodles, seasoning packets discarded

6 ounces sugar snap peas or snow peas, trimmed

1 scallion, white and green parts, thinly sliced

1 medium carrot, shredded

1 tablespoon Asian dark sesame oil

Hot chili oil, for serving

MAKES 2 TO 3 SERVINGS

Southeast Asian Shrimp Soup with Lemongrass and Chiles

Chicken soup has a reputation as a cure for the common cold, but I nominate this head-clearing broth. Thai and Vietnamese cuisines both have a version. Mine has plenty of spice from the chiles, plus the citrus note of lemongrass.

IN A MEDIUM SAUCEPAN, bring the shrimp shells, broth, and 3 cups water to a boil over high heat. Reduce the heat to low and simmer for 20 minutes. Strain the broth into a bowl. Set aside.

IN A LARGE DUTCH OVEN OR FLAMEPROOF CASSEROLE, heat the oil over medium heat. Add the shallots, lemongrass (if using lime zest, add with the lime juice in step 3), ginger, chile pepper, and garlic. Cook, stirring often, until the shallots are softened, about 1 minute. Add the strained broth and bring to a boil over high heat. Reduce the heat to low and simmer for 5 minutes.

ADD THE SHRIMP, bamboo shoots, tomatoes, lime juice (and lime zest, if using), fish sauce, and sugar. Cook just until the shrimps turn pink and firm, 2 to 3 minutes (the soup does not have to return to a boil). Serve hot, topped with the bean sprouts and cilantro.

1 pound medium shrimp, peeled (use the shells in the broth) and deveined

3 cups chicken broth, preferably home-made, or use low-sodium canned broth

2 tablespoons vegetable oil

⅓ cup chopped shallots

3 tablespoons minced lemongrass, tender bulb part only, or grated zest of 1 lime

1 tablespoon thinly sliced fresh ginger

1 tablespoon minced small chile pepper, such as jalapeño

2 garlic cloves, minced

1 can (8 ounces) sliced bamboo shoots, rinsed and drained

2 large ripe tomatoes, seeded and coarsely chopped

¼ cup fresh lime juice

3 tablespoons Asian fish sauce (see page 37)

1 tablespoon sugar

2 cups fresh bean sprouts

2 tablespoons chopped fresh cilantro

MAKES 6 SERVINGS

1 pound medium shrimp, peeled and deveined

1 tablespoon soy sauce

1 tablespoon Asian dark sesame oil

1 tablespoon dry sherry

1 tablespoon cornstarch

1 teaspoon minced fresh ginger

¼ teaspoon salt

⅛ teaspoon freshly ground pepper

¼ cup finely chopped scallions

36 square won ton wrappers

5 cups chicken broth, preferably home-made, or low-sodium canned broth

4 ounces fresh spinach leaves, tough stems discarded and cut into ¼-inch-wide strips

MAKES 6 SERVINGS

Shrimp and Spinach Won Ton Soup

Nothing beats homemade won tons, especially when filled with this delicate shrimp stuffing. High-quality won ton wrappers are worth seeking out—the best are made from just flour, eggs, and water and no preservatives. Make a habit of buying them at a well-stocked Asian market; you can freeze them for up to 6 months.

IN A FOOD PROCESSOR, pulse the shrimp, soy sauce, sesame oil, sherry, cornstarch, ginger, salt, and pepper until very finely chopped. Add the scallions and pulse until combined. Transfer the mixture to a small bowl.

PLACE 1 WON TON WRAPPER ON A FLAT WORK SURFACE, point up. Moisten the edges of the wrapper with water. Place 1 teaspoon of the shrimp mixture in the center of the wrapper. Fold up the wrapper from bottom to top, enclosing the filling, with the points at the top. Press the edges to seal. Bring the sides together to meet, dab with water, and press to seal. Transfer the filled won ton to a wax paper–lined baking sheet. Repeat with the remaining wrappers and filling.

BRING A LARGE POT OF LIGHTLY SALTED WATER to a boil over high heat. Add the won tons and return to a boil. Add 1 cup cold water and allow the water to return to a boil again. Using a slotted skimmer, transfer the won tons to a large bowl of cold water. (The won tons can be prepared up to 1 hour ahead, covered, and refrigerated in the cold water.)

IN A LARGE POT, BRING THE BROTH TO A BOIL over high heat. Stir in the spinach and cook until tender, about 1 minute. Drain the won tons and add them to the soup. Cook until the won tons are heated through, about 2 minutes. Serve immediately.

Beer and Spice Shrimp
with Bumpy Mayonnaise

Shrimp and beer are old buddies—the bitter beer complements the sweet shrimp. I always add a handful of spices to the pot, which soften enough to stir into a mustard and mayonnaise dip.

BRING THE BEER, CORIANDER SEEDS, mustard seeds, cloves, bay leaf, red pepper, and garlic to a simmer over medium heat. Cover, reduce the heat to low, and simmer until the seeds are softened, about 10 minutes

INCREASE THE HEAT TO HIGH and bring the liquid to a full boil. Add the shrimp and cover. Cook until the shrimps turn pink and firm, 2 to 3 minutes (the liquid does not have to return to a boil). Using a slotted spoon, transfer the shrimps to a large bowl and cover to keep warm.

TO MAKE THE MUSTARD-MAYONNAISE, strain the cooking liquid into a wire sieve, discarding the garlic, whole cloves, and bay leaf. Transfer the remaining spices to a small bowl. Add the mayonnaise and mustard and stir. Season with hot pepper sauce.

SERVE THE SHRIMP along with the mayonnaise, for dipping. Peel the shrimp at the table.

1 bottle (12 ounces) lager beer
1 teaspoon coriander seeds
1 teaspoon mustard seeds
6 whole cloves
1 bay leaf
¼ teaspoon crushed red pepper
2 large garlic cloves, crushed
2 pounds medium shrimp, unpeeled

BUMPY MUSTARD-MAYONNAISE
Drained spices from cooking shrimp
1 cup mayonnaise
2 tablespoons Dijon mustard
Hot red pepper sauce, to taste

MAKES 4 SERVINGS

2 medium onions, sliced

2 medium celery ribs with leaves, sliced

1 head garlic, separated into cloves and peeled

¼ cup Shrimp Boil Spices (recipe follows)

1 tablespoon salt

2 pounds small new potatoes, scrubbed, or medium red potatoes, scrubbed and cut into 1-inch cubes

1 pound spicy smoked sausage, such as kielbasa or hot links, cut into 2-inch pieces

6 ears corn, husks and silks removed

3 pounds medium shrimp

Melted butter, for serving

Lemon wedges, for serving

MAKES 6 TO 8 SERVINGS

Low Country Shrimp, Sausage, and Corn Boil

You'll need a huge stockpot to make this specialty of the South Carolina shore—and plenty of napkins! Instead of using store-bought crab boil spices, make your own.

IN A LARGE STOCKPOT, bring 4 quarts water, the onions, celery, garlic, Shrimp Boil Spices, and salt to a boil over high heat. Add the potatoes and reduce the heat to medium. Partially cover and simmer until the potatoes are almost done, about 20 minutes.

ADD THE SAUSAGE AND CORN, increase the heat to high, and return to a full boil. Boil for 2 minutes. Add the shrimp and cook until pink and firm, 2 to 3 minutes (the liquid does not have to return to a boil).

USING A LARGE SKIMMER AND TONGS, transfer the shrimps, sausage, potatoes, and corn to separate platters and bowls. (This is easier than trying to drain the stockpot.) Serve immediately, with bowls of melted butter and the lemon wedges on the side.

Shrimp Boil Spices

Mix 2 tablespoons yellow mustard seeds, 1 teaspoon black peppercorns, 1 teaspoon coriander seeds, 1 teaspoon *each* dried thyme, dill seed, and celery seed, 6 allspice berries, 6 crumbled dried chile peppers (or ½ teaspoon crushed red pepper), and 2 crumbled bay leaves. Makes about ¼ cup.

Spicy Steamed Shrimp with Chesapeake Bay Spices

This method of cooking shrimp ensures finger-licking results—the shrimp must be peeled at the table, and the seasoning gets all over your fingers. Vary the steaming liquid according your mood. Many commercial seasoning blends are available, but I prefer to make my own, which is less salty than the supermarket versions. If necessary, grind whole spices in an electric coffee grinder. Use the seasoning in coatings for fried chicken and fish fillets, or in any steamed food, or—my favorite —sprinkled on buttered popcorn.

2 cups water, flat beer, or dry white wine

3 pounds medium shrimp

3 tablespoons Chesapeake Bay Seasoning (recipe follows)

MAKES 6 SERVINGS

PLACE A COLLAPSIBLE STEAMER BASKET in the bottom of a large pot. Add enough of the liquid to almost reach the bottom of the steamer. Bring to a boil over high heat. Add the shrimp in layers, sprinkling each layer with the seasoning. Cover tightly and cook until the shrimps turn pink and firm, about 3 minutes. Serve immediately.

Chesapeake Bay Seasoning

Mix 2 teaspoons salt, 1 teaspoon *each* cayenne, ground celery seed, sweet Hungarian paprika, dry mustard, ground black pepper, ground bay leaf, and ¼ teaspoon *each* ground allspice, ground ginger, grated nutmeg, ground cardamom, and ground cinnamon. Makes about ¼ cup. (The seasoning will keep indefinitely in a tightly covered container, stored at room temperature in a cool, dark place.)

Shrimp from the Skillet

**SHRIMP WITH ASPARAGUS
AND ALMONDS**

Out of the Frying Pan

Sautéing shrimp in a skillet is one of the best ways to get supper on the table fast. Shrimp should be cooked in under 3 minutes in order to retain its sweet flavor and crisp-juicy texture—no one likes dried-out, over-cooked shrimp.

A large nonstick skillet with a 12-inch diameter is an indispensable kitchen utensil. It is big enough to cook most foods without crowding. Generally, you want browned meats and chicken, since the caramel-ized surfaces add flavors, and if the food is crowded into too-small a skillet, it creates excess steam, which hinders the browning process. Of course, you don't want to brown shrimp—it would be overcooked by that time. But you still should not crowd the skillet: the shrimp would release its juices too soon. Another, practical reason for cooking in a large skillet is that it will hold enough food for four to six servings.

There are quite a few Asian stir-fries in this chapter, but you don't have to take out the wok. The large skillet works just as well, with the added advantage that you don't have to worry about juggling the wok on the burner ring. If you do a lot of stir-frying, a flat-bottomed stir-fry pan is a nice addition to your kitchen equipment, but not imperative.

When stir-frying in a wok, the cook is usually instructed to heat the wok over high heat, then add the oil. This ensures that the oil will be very hot when the food is added, searing it more effectively. However, nonstick surfaces should not be exposed to a high flame. When cooking in a nonstick skillet, use medium to medium-high heat.

Shrimp with Asparagus and Almonds

From the Cantonese shrimp lexicon, here is a fast stir-fry that celebrates the delicious pairing of asparagus and shrimp. If your asparagus is on the thick side (over 1/2 inch), cut it lengthwise in half before cutting crosswise into lengths; that way it will cook in the allotted time.

IN A MEDIUM BOWL, MIX THE BROTH, soy sauce, sherry, sugar, salt, and pepper. Add the cornstarch and stir to dissolve. Set aside.

HEAT A LARGE (12-INCH) NONSTICK SKILLET over medium-high heat. Add the almonds and toast, stirring occasionally, until lightly browned, 2 to 3 minutes. Transfer to a plate and set aside.

HEAT THE SAME SKILLET OVER MEDIUM-HIGH HEAT, add the oil, and swirl to coat the inside of the skillet with the oil. Add the scallions and ginger and stir-fry until fragrant, about 30 seconds. Add the asparagus and stir-fry for 1 minute. Stir in the shrimp and cover. Cook until the shrimps are pink and firm, about 2 minutes. Add the soy sauce mixture, bring to a boil, and cook until thickened, about 30 seconds. Sprinkle with the toasted almonds. Serve immediately.

½ cup chicken broth, preferably home-made, or low-sodium canned broth

2 tablespoons soy sauce

1 tablespoon dry sherry

1 teaspoon sugar

¼ teaspoon salt

¼ teaspoon freshly ground pepper

2 teaspoons cornstarch

½ cup slivered almonds

2 tablespoons vegetable oil

3 scallions, white and green parts, chopped

2 teaspoons minced fresh ginger

1 pound thin asparagus, spears trimmed and cut into ½-inch lengths

1½ pounds medium shrimp, peeled and deveined

MAKES 4 SERVINGS

TARTAR SAUCE

1 cup mayonnaise

2 scallions, white and green parts, minced

2 tablespoons finely chopped cornichons (tiny French pickles) or sour dill pickles

2 tablespoons finely chopped rinsed capers

2 tablespoons finely chopped fresh parsley

1 pound medium shrimp, peeled and deveined

¾ cup dried bread crumbs

¼ cup Tartar Sauce

2 large eggs, beaten

1 scallion, white and green parts, finely chopped

1½ teaspoons Dijon mustard

½ teaspoon Worcestershire sauce

⅛ teaspoon hot pepper sauce

Nonstick vegetable oil spray

MAKES 4 SHRIMP CAKES

Shrimp Cakes with Homemade Tartar Sauce

Serve these shrimp cakes on their own with cole slaw and sliced tomatoes for a simple supper, or turn them into sandwiches on toasted sesame rolls. Homemade tartar sauce elevates these into a class above the ordinary.

TO MAKE THE SAUCE, combine all the ingredients in a small bowl. Cover and refrigerate to blend the flavors, at least 1 hour. (The sauce can be prepared up to 3 days ahead.)

IN A FOOD PROCESSOR, pulse the shrimp until very finely chopped. Add the bread crumbs, Tartar Sauce, eggs, scallion, mustard, Worcestershire, and hot pepper sauce. Transfer to a medium bowl. Rinse your hands with water and form into four 3-inch-wide cakes.

SPRAY A LARGE (12-INCH) NONSTICK SKILLET with vegetable oil and heat over medium-high heat. Cook the cakes until the undersides are golden brown, about 3 minutes. Turn and brown the other sides, about 2 minutes. Serve immediately, with the remaining Tartar Sauce on the side.

Sichuan Shrimp with Cashews

If you visit an Asian grocer and keep ingredients like chili paste, sesame oil, and black vinegar on hand, you can mix up this wonderful stir-fry of shrimp, bell pepper, and cashews in a spicy sauce in no time. Stir-fries used to intimidate me, until I learned that some of the ingredients are made into a marinade, and more of the same ingredients go into the sauce.

FOR A MARINADE, in a medium bowl, mix 2 tablespoons of the soy sauce, the egg white, and cornstarch with a fork until the cornstarch dissolves. Add the shrimp and toss to coat. Let stand for 15 to 30 minutes.

FOR A SAUCE, in a small bowl, stir the remaining 3 tablespoons soy sauce, sherry, vinegar, brown sugar, sesame oil, chili paste, and salt to dissolve the sugar. Set aside.

HEAT A LARGE (12-INCH) NONSTICK SKILLET over medium-high heat. Add 2 tablespoons of the oil, swirl to coat the skillet, heat the oil until very hot. Add the dried peppers and stir-fry until fragrant, about 15 seconds. Add the shrimps and stir-fry until the coating is set, about 1 minute. (The shrimps will seem slightly underdone at this point.) Using a slotted spoon, transfer the shrimps and chiles to a plate and set aside.

ADD THE REMAINING 1 TABLESPOON OIL to the skillet and heat until very hot. Add the bell pepper and stir-fry until softened, about 2 minutes. Add the scallions, ginger, and garlic, and stir-fry until fragrant, about 30 seconds. Return the shrimp to the skillet and add the cashews. Stir in the soy sauce mixture and bring to a boil. Cook until the shrimps are cooked through, about 1 minute. Serve immediately, with the rice.

5 tablespoons soy sauce

1 large egg white

1½ tablespoons cornstarch

1½ pounds medium shrimp, peeled and deveined

2 tablespoons dry sherry

1 tablespoon Chinese black vinegar or balsamic vinegar

2 teaspoons light brown sugar

2 teaspoons Asian dark sesame oil

¾ teaspoon Chinese chile paste with garlic or ½ teaspoon hot red pepper sauce

¼ teaspoon salt

3 tablespoons vegetable oil

6 small dried chile peppers

1 large red bell pepper, seeded and cut into ½-inch squares

3 scallions, white and green parts, chopped

1½ tablespoons minced fresh ginger

1 large garlic clove, minced

1 cup (5 ounces) roasted salted cashews

Hot cooked rice, for serving

MAKES 4 SERVINGS

Buttermilk Biscuits with Low Country Shrimp and Ham

In South Carolina, creamed shrimp on grits is considered the best breakfast on earth. I think it's even better when made with slivers of Smithfield ham and spooned over freshly baked biscuits. Use a blend of cake and bleached all-purpose flours to simulate soft wheat flour, like White Lily, which all Southerners know makes the best biscuits. Serve this for Sunday brunch with individual bowls of fresh fruit salad.

PREHEAT THE OVEN TO 400° F.

TO MAKE THE BISCUITS, sift the cake flour, all-purpose flour, cream of tartar, baking soda, and salt into a medium bowl. Using a pastry blender or 2 forks, cut in the butter until the mixture resembles coarse meal. Stirring with a fork, gradually pour as much buttermilk as needed to make a soft dough. Knead the dough lightly in the bowl just until it comes together. Do not overwork the dough. Turn out onto a lightly floured work surface. Roll into a ½-inch-thick circle. Using a 3-inch round biscuit cutter, cut out biscuits and place them on an ungreased baking sheet. Gather up the scraps and quickly and gently knead them back into a flat disk. Roll and cut out more biscuits and place on the baking sheet. (You will have 7 biscuits, which is one more than needed, the extra one being the cook's treat.) Bake until the biscuits are golden brown, 18 to 20 minutes. Remove from the oven, and wrap in a clean kitchen towel to keep warm. (The biscuits can be prepared up to 2 hours ahead, cooled at room temperature, and reheated. Wrap the biscuits loosely in foil and bake in a preheated 350° F. oven for 10 to 15 minutes, or until heated through.)

(CONTINUED)

BUTTERMILK BISCUITS

1 cup cake flour

1 cup bleached all-purpose flour

2 teaspoons cream of tartar

1 teaspoon baking soda

½ teaspoon salt

8 tablespoons (1 stick) unsalted butter, chilled and cut into ½-inch cubes

¾ cup plus 2 tablespoons buttermilk

1 tablespoon unsalted butter

3 ounces (¼-inch thick) Smithfield ham, Black Forest ham, or prosciutto, sliced ¼ inch thick, cut into ¼-inch-wide slivers

1½ pounds medium shrimp, peeled (use the shells in the stock) and deveined

½ cup chopped scallions, white and green parts

3 cups Shrimp Stock (page 16)

½ cup dry vermouth or additional broth

2 cups heavy cream

2 teaspoons chopped fresh tarragon or 1 teaspoon dried tarragon

¼ teaspoon salt

Hot red pepper sauce, to taste

MAKES 6 SERVINGS

IN A LARGE NONSTICK SKILLET heat the butter over medium-high heat. Add the ham and cook until it begins to brown, about 1 minute. Add the shrimp and scallions and cook, stirring occasionally, until the shrimps turn pink and firm, 2 to 3 minutes. Using a slotted spoon, transfer the shrimps and scallions to a bowl. Set aside.

ADD THE BROTH AND VERMOUTH and bring to a boil over high heat. Boil until reduced by half, about 8 minutes. Add the cream, tarragon, and any accumulated juices from the bowl of shrimp. Boil until the sauce reduces enough to lightly coat a wooden spoon, about 5 minutes. Return the shrimp and scallions to the skillet, just to reheat, about 1 minute. Season with the salt and hot pepper sauce.

TO SERVE, SLICE THE BISCUITS in half horizontally. On each plate, place a biscuit, cut sides up. Spoon equal amounts of the creamed shrimp evenly over the biscuits. Serve immediately.

Shrimp Diane

Steak Diane is cooked with a savory sauce that is too good to reserve for red meat—its zesty flavors also complement shrimp.

IN A LARGE (12-INCH) NONSTICK SKILLET, heat 1 tablespoon of the butter over medium-high heat. Add half of the shrimp and cook until pink and firm, 2 to 3 minutes. Transfer to a bowl and cover to keep warm. Repeat with another tablespoon of butter and the remaining shrimp.

IN THE SAME SKILLET, heat 1 tablespoon butter over medium-high heat. Add the shallots and stir until softened, about 1 minute. Add the wine, lemon juice, mustard, Worcestershire, and pepper. Bring to a simmer, scraping up the browned bits on the bottom of the skillet with a wooden spoon.

REMOVE FROM THE HEAT. Add the remaining 3 tablespoons butter and the parsley and stir until the butter melts. Return the shrimp to the skillet and stir to coat with the sauce. Serve immediately.

6 tablespoons (¾ stick) unsalted butter

2 pounds medium shrimp, peeled and deveined

⅓ cup minced shallots

½ cup dry white wine

2 tablespoons fresh lemon juice

1 tablespoon Dijon mustard

1 tablespoon Worcestershire sauce

¼ teaspoon freshly ground pepper

2 tablespoons finely chopped parsley

MAKES 4 SERVINGS

TOMATILLO SAUCE

1 can (26 ounces) tomatillos, drained and rinsed (see Note)

¼ cup chopped onion

¼ cup chopped fresh cilantro

1 jalapeño, seeded and chopped

2 garlic cloves, chopped

½ teaspoon dried oregano

¼ teaspoon salt

Pinch of sugar

2 tablespoons vegetable oil

½ cup heavy cream

12 corn tortillas (6 inches), torn into quarters

Nonstick vegetable oil spray

1½ cups Tomatillo Sauce

1 cup chicken broth, preferably home-made, or low-sodium canned broth

¾ pound medium shrimp, peeled, deveined, and coarsely chopped

¾ cup shredded Monterey jack cheese

MAKES 4 TO 6 SERVINGS

Shrimp Chilaquiles Suizas

Enchiladas suizas (Swiss enchiladas) have a cream-enriched tomatillo sauce. The Mexicans must have named them to commemorate the Swiss fondness for anything made with dairy products (which I can confirm since my grandmother was born in neighboring Liechtenstein). Chilaquiles are kind of a skillet enchilada casserole, traditionally prepared with fried leftover tortillas. In this country, most cooks will prefer my lighter, oven-dried tortillas.

TO MAKE THE SAUCE, combine the tomatillos, onion, cilantro, jalapeño, garlic, oregano, salt, and sugar in a food processor and process until smooth. (The sauce can also be prepared, in batches, in a blender.)

IN A MEDIUM NONSTICK SKILLET, heat the oil over medium heat. Add the sauce (it will splatter) and cream. Bring to a boil. Reduce the heat to low and simmer, stirring often, until slightly thickened, 3 to 5 minutes.

POSITION THE OVEN RACKS in the top third and center of the oven and preheat to 350° F.

ARRANGE THE TORTILLA PIECES on baking sheets and spray lightly with the vegetable oil. Bake, stirring occasionally, until they feel leathery but not hard, about 10 minutes.

POSITION THE BROILER RACK about 6 inches from the source of heat and preheat the broiler.

RETURN THE SAUCE IN THE SKILLET to a boil over medium-high heat. Add the tortilla pieces, a few at a time, pushing under the sauce with a spoon. When all the tortillas have been added, reduce the heat to low and simmer until the tortillas have absorbed the sauce, about 5 minutes. Sprinkle with the shrimp, and then the Monterey jack. Broil until the shrimps are pink and firm, and the cheese has melted, about 3 minutes. Serve immediately.

NOTE: Canned tomatillos are available at Hispanic markets and by mail order (page 161). The sauce can also be prepared with fresh tomatillos. Husk 1¾ pounds fresh tomatillos. Simmer in a large saucepan of lightly salted water over medium heat until tender, 6 to 10 minutes, depending on the size of the tomatillos. If your tomatillos are not all the same size (which happens often), as the smaller tomatillos become tender, remove them from the simmering water with a slotted spoon. Do not let the tomatillos cook at a hard boil, or they may break apart. Drain carefully and rinse under cold water.

¼ cup soy sauce

2 tablespoons dry sherry

2 tablespoons cornstarch

1½ pounds large shrimp, peeled and deveined

1 cup chicken broth, preferably home-made, or low-sodium canned broth

2 tablespoons rice vinegar

2 tablespoons sugar

½ teaspoon salt

2 tablespoons vegetable oil

2 tablespoons minced fresh ginger

1 jalapeño, seeded and minced

2 garlic cloves, minced

1 medium red onion, thinly sliced into half-moons

1 medium red bell pepper, seeded and cut into ¼-inch-thick strips

2 medium mangoes (1 pound), pitted, peeled, and cut into ½-inch-wide strips (see Note)

MAKES 4 SERVINGS

Sweet-and-Sour Shrimp with Mango and Ginger

For those who like the combination of shrimp and fruit, here's a colorful stir-fry. Mangoes reach their peak during the last spring months.

IN A MEDIUM BOWL, combine 2 tablespoons of the soy sauce and the sherry. Add 1 tablespoon of the cornstarch and stir to dissolve. Stir in the shrimp. Cover and let stand for at least 15 minutes and up to 30 minutes.

IN A SMALL BOWL, combine the broth, the remaining 2 tablespoons soy sauce, the vinegar, sugar, and salt. Add the remaining 1 tablespoon cornstarch and stir to dissolve. Set aside.

HEAT A LARGE (12-INCH) SKILLET over medium-high heat. Add the oil, swirl to coat the skillet, and heat until the oil is very hot. Add the ginger, jalapeño, and garlic and stir until very fragrant, about 30 seconds. Add the red onion and bell pepper. Stir-fry until the onion is softened, about 3 minutes.

DRAIN THE SHRIMP. Add to the skillet along with the mango strips. Cook, turning gently so the mango strips don't break up, just until the shrimps begin to turn pink and firm, about 1 minute. Add the broth mixture, bring to a boil, and cook until thickened, about 1 minute. Serve immediately.

NOTE: To pit and peel a mango, choose a ripe mango that yields to gentle pressure (just like a ripe peach). The mango pit is long and flat, and runs vertically through the fruit, so the trick is to cut the flesh away without hitting the pit. Lay the mango on a work surface, plump side down. Using a sharp, thin-bladed knife, slice off the top third of the mango, cutting around the pit. Turn the mango over and slice off the other side. Using a large spoon, scoop out the mango flesh in 1 piece from the peel.

Spanish Shrimp and Red Peppers in Garlic Sauce

What we would call appetizers or hors d'oeuvres are turned into an art form called tapas in Spain. One of the most popular is shrimp served in a gutsy garlic sauce. My main-course version is bolstered with vegetables and served over Saffron Rice.

IN A LARGE (12-INCH) NONSTICK SKILLET, heat the oil over medium heat. Add the onion, bell pepper, and garlic. Cook, stirring often, until the pepper is softened, about 5 minutes.

STIR IN THE PAPRIKA. Add the broth, sherry, lemon juice, and pepper and bring to a boil. Reduce the heat to medium-low and cover. Simmer for 3 minutes. Add the shrimp and cook for 1 minute.

TRANSFER ABOUT ¼ CUP OF THE COOKING LIQUID to a small bowl. Add the cornstarch and stir to dissolve. Pour into the skillet and cook until the sauce thickens and the shrimps are pink and firm, about 1 minute. Season with the salt. Serve, spooned over the Saffron Rice.

Saffron Rice

In a medium saucepan, bring 3 cups chicken broth, 1½ cups long-grain rice, ½ teaspoon salt, and ⅛ teaspoon crushed saffron threads to a boil over high heat. Reduce the heat to low and cover tightly. Simmer until the rice is tender and absorbs the liquid, about 15 minutes. Remove from the heat and let stand, covered, for 5 minutes before serving.

1 tablespoon extra virgin olive oil

1 medium onion, chopped

1 large red bell pepper, seeded and chopped

6 large garlic cloves, minced

¾ teaspoon sweet Spanish or Hungarian paprika

1½ cups chicken broth, preferably home-made, or low-sodium canned broth

3 tablespoons dry sherry

1 tablespoon fresh lemon juice

¼ teaspoon freshly ground pepper

1½ pounds medium shrimp, peeled and deveined

2 teaspoons cornstarch

¼ teaspoon salt

Saffron Rice (recipe follows)

MAKES 4 SERVINGS

ROMESCO SAUCE

⅓ cup sliced almonds

½ cup plus 2 tablespoons olive oil

1 small onion, finely chopped

2 large garlic cloves, minced

2 fresh plum tomatoes, peeled, seeded, and coarsely chopped, or 2 canned tomatoes

1 tablespoon tomato paste

½ teaspoon salt

⅛ teaspoon cayenne, or to taste

1½ pounds medium shrimp, deveined through the shell if desired

2 tablespoons extra virgin olive oil

1 teaspoon kosher salt

MAKES 4 SERVINGS

Grilled Shrimp a la Plancha with Romesco Sauce

In Spanish, *a la plancha* means on a grill, or grilled, which could be pan-grilled in a skillet as often as cooked over charcoal. There's no easier way to cook shrimp—toss with oil and coarse salt and sear. Since it takes a couple of minutes to cook the shrimp, it's best to do it in small batches and serve from the pan. It is important to use shell-on shrimp; the shell protects the flesh from the heat of the skillet.

TO MAKE THE SAUCE, heat a medium skillet over medium heat. Add the almonds and cook, stirring almost constantly, until toasted, about 2 minutes. Transfer to a plate and let cool.

ADD 2 TABLESPOONS OF THE OIL to the skillet and heat. Add the onion and cook until golden, about 3 minutes. Add the garlic and stir for 1 minute. Transfer to a blender or a food processor. Add the almonds, tomatoes, and tomato paste. With the machine running, gradually pour in the remaining ½ cup oil and process until thickened. Season with the salt and cayenne. Transfer to a bowl, cover, and let stand for at least 1 hour to allow the flavors to blend. (The sauce can be prepared up to 2 days ahead, covered, and refrigerated. Bring to room temperature before serving.)

IN A MEDIUM BOWL, TOSS THE SHRIMP with the oil, and then the salt. Heat a large, heavy skillet or ridged grilling skillet (preferably cast iron) over medium-high heat. Add the shrimp in batches without crowding. Cook, turning once, just until the shells turn orange, 2 to 3 minutes. Serve immediately with the romesco sauce for dipping.

Shrimp Peacemaker Sandwich

The legend of the peacemaker sandwich tells how miscreant husbands would bring home a warm sandwich stuffed with fried seafood as an apology to their angry (and, one assumes, hungry) wives. The same sandwich, with minor variations, is served up and down the Eastern seaboard, too.

¾ pound medium shrimp, peeled and deveined

2 large eggs, beaten

½ cup dried bread crumbs

Vegetable shortening, for deep-frying

4 long, soft rolls, split lengthwise

Rémoulade Sauce (page 24)

1½ cups shredded iceberg lettuce

1 ripe large beefsteak tomato, thinly sliced

MAKES 2 SANDWICHES

HAVE READY 2 SHALLOW DISHES, one with the beaten eggs and one with the bread crumbs. Dip the shrimps one at a time in the eggs, letting the excess run back into the bowl. Roll in the bread crumbs. Place on a wire cake rack set over a baking sheet. Refrigerate to set the coating, at least 1 hour and up to 2 hours.

IN A LARGE, HEAVY SKILLET, melt enough shortening over medium-high heat to come 1½ inches up the side of the skillet and heat to 360° F. (An electric skillet works best.) Deep-fry the shrimps in batches until golden, 2 to 3 minutes. Transfer to the wire rack to drain.

SPREAD THE ROLLS WITH RÉMOULADE SAUCE, then fill with equal amounts of fried shrimp, lettuce, and tomatoes. Serve immediately.

CAPE COD SHRIMP SANDWICH:
Substitute Tartar Sauce (page 84) for the Rémoulade Sauce.

Shrimp au Poivre

When you need an impressive main course in a hurry, try this peppery shrimp sauté, finished with a Cognac and cream sauce. Serve it with a colorful vegetable mélange (such as baby carrots and sugar snap peas) and oven-roasted new potatoes.

IN A LARGE (12-INCH) NONSTICK SKILLET, heat 1 tablespoon of the butter over medium heat. Add the shrimp, salt, and pepper. Cook until pink and firm, 2 to 3 minutes. Transfer to a plate and set aside.

IN THE SAME SKILLET, heat the remaining 1 tablespoon butter. Add the shallots and cook, stirring often, until softened, about 2 minutes. Add the Cognac and cook until almost evaporated. Stir in the heavy cream and increase the heat to high. Cook until reduced by half, about 2 minutes.

RETURN THE SHRIMP TO THE SKILLET and toss to coat with the sauce. Serve immediately, sprinkled with the chives.

2 tablespoons unsalted butter

1½ pounds large shrimp, peeled and deveined

¼ teaspoon salt

¼ teaspoon whole black peppercorns, crushed in a mortar or under a heavy skillet, or more to taste

2 tablespoons minced shallots

2 tablespoons Cognac or brandy

1 cup heavy cream

1 tablespoon finely chopped fresh chives or parsley

MAKES 4 SERVINGS

Shrimp and Summer Vegetable Sauté

Other summer vegetables—green beans, red bell peppers, celery, chile peppers—can also be added to this sauté according to the cook's whim. Serve with couscous or orzo.

3 tablespoons extra virgin olive oil

1 pound medium shrimp, peeled and deveined

1 medium zucchini, scrubbed and cut into ½-inch cubes

3 scallions, white and green parts, chopped

1 garlic clove, minced

4 ripe plum tomatoes, seeded and cut into ½-inch cubes

1 cup fresh or thawed frozen corn kernels

½ teaspoon salt

¼ teaspoon freshly ground pepper

½ cup dry white wine

2 teaspoons cornstarch

⅔ cup chicken broth, preferably homemade, or use low-sodium canned broth

2 tablespoons chopped fresh basil

MAKES 4 TO 6 SERVINGS

IN A LARGE (12-INCH) NONSTICK SKILLET, heat 1 tablespoon of the oil over medium-high heat. Add the shrimp and cook until pink and firm, 2 to 3 minutes. Transfer to a bowl and cover to keep warm.

ADD THE REMAINING OIL to the skillet and heat. Add the zucchini and cook until lightly browned, stirring occasionally, about 5 minutes. Add the scallions and garlic and cook until the scallions are wilted, about 2 minutes. Add the tomatoes, corn, salt, and pepper and cook until heated through, about 3 minutes. Add the wine and cook until reduced by half, about 1 minute.

IN A SMALL BOWL, add the cornstarch to the broth and stir to dissolve. Pour into the skillet and cook until thickened, about 1 minute. Stir in the shrimp and the basil. Serve immediately.

Indian Shrimp with Zucchini, Cilantro, and Coriander

This mildly spiced Indian dish comes together in no time. It uses both coriander seeds and fresh cilantro, which are from the same plant but with entirely different flavors. For the best flavor, grind coriander seeds in a mortar or an electric spice grinder.

IN A LARGE (12-INCH) NONSTICK SKILLET, heat the oil over medium heat. Add the zucchini, onion, ginger, jalapeño, and garlic. Cook, stirring occasionally, until the onions are golden, 5 to 6 minutes.

ADD THE GROUND CORIANDER, TURMERIC, AND SALT. Stir until the spices are fragrant, about 30 seconds. Add the shrimp. Cook just until the shrimps begin to turn opaque, about 1 minute.

ADD THE COCONUT MILK AND LEMON JUICE and bring to a boil. Cook until thickened, 1 to 2 minutes. Stir in the cilantro. Serve immediately, with the rice.

2 tablespoons vegetable oil

2 medium zucchini, scrubbed and cut into ½-inch cubes

1 medium onion, chopped

1 tablespoon minced fresh ginger

1 jalapeño, seeded and minced

2 garlic cloves, minced

1½ teaspoons ground coriander

½ teaspoon turmeric

¼ teaspoon salt

1½ pounds medium shrimp, peeled and deveined

½ cup canned coconut milk

3 tablespoons fresh lemon juice

3 tablespoons chopped fresh cilantro

Hot cooked rice, for serving

MAKES 4 SERVINGS

Shrimp on Pasta and Rice

Fettuccine with Shrimp, Artichokes, and Porcini Mushrooms
Spaghetti with Shrimp, Anchovies, and Bread Crumbs
Fettuccine with Shrimp, Asparagus, and Mint
Spaghetti with Shrimp, Capers, and Garlic
Spaghetti with Shrimp in Garlicky Wine Sauce
Fettuccine with Shrimp, Pan-Roasted Peppers, and Balsamic Vinegar
Spaghetti with Shrimp in Spicy Sicilian Sauce
Shrimp Agnolotti in Ginger Sauce
Spaghetti with Shrimp, Zucchini, and Prosciutto
Indonesian Fried Noodles with Shrimp and Ham
Moroccan-Spiced Shrimp on Fruited Couscous
Curried Rice Noodles with Shrimp
Southeast Asian Basil Shrimp with Rice Sticks
Risotto Primavera with Shrimp
Shrimp Jambalaya
Shrimp and Green Bean Pilau
Malaysian Fried Rice

**SOUTHEAST ASIAN BASIL SHRIMP
WITH RICE STICKS**

½ cup (½ ounce) dried porcini
    mushrooms

1 large lemon, cut in half

6 medium (8 ounces *each*) artichokes

2 tablespoons olive oil

1 medium onion, chopped

1 garlic clove, minced

8 ounces cremini or white button mush-
    rooms, thinly sliced

1 cup heavy cream

1 pound medium shrimp, peeled and
    deveined

¾ teaspoon salt

½ teaspoon freshly ground pepper

1 pound fettuccine

2 tablespoons chopped fresh basil

MAKES 4 TO 6 SERVINGS

Fettuccine with Shrimp, Artichokes, and Porcini Mushrooms

The elegant combination of shrimp, artichokes, and porcini mushrooms makes this a fine pasta for company. Trimming fresh artichokes is a labor of love, but practice will make perfect.

IN A SMALL BOWL, soak the dried mushrooms in 1 cup hot water until softened, about 30 minutes. Lift out the mushrooms, rinse quickly under cold water to remove grit, and coarsely chop. Place the mushrooms in a bowl. Strain the soaking liquid through a paper towel–lined sieve into the bowl and set aside.

SQUEEZE THE LEMON INTO A MEDIUM BOWL filled with 1 quart cold water. Working with 1 artichoke at a time, snap off and discard the tough dark green leaves, revealing the light green cone of tender leaves. Using a sharp paring knife, cut off the leafy cone where it meets the thick artichoke base and discard the leaves. Dip the artichoke into lemon water as you work to prevent discoloration. Trim away all of the dark green skin from the base and stem (if attached). Use the tip of the knife to cut out any purple leaves and the hairy choke from the center of the base and discard. Cut the artichoke heart into ¼-inch-thick slices. Place in the lemon water. Repeat with the remaining artichokes.

IN A LARGE (12-INCH) NONSTICK SKILLET, heat the oil over medium heat. Add the onion and cook, stirring often, until softened, about 3 minutes. Add the garlic and cook for 1 minute. Drain the sliced artichoke heart slices and add to the skillet. Cook, stirring occasionally, for 2 minutes. Add the fresh mushrooms and cook, stirring occasionally, until the mushrooms wilt, about 5 minutes. Add the chopped porcini mushrooms and their soaking liquid. Bring to a boil, reduce the heat to medium-low, and cover. Simmer until the artichoke slices are tender, 20 to 25 minutes.

ADD THE HEAVY CREAM AND BRING TO A BOIL. Cook until reduced by half, about 3 minutes. Add the shrimp, salt, and pepper. Cook, stirring occasionally, until pink and firm, about 3 minutes. Remove from the heat and cover to keep warm.

MEANWHILE, BRING A LARGE POT OF LIGHTLY SALTED WATER to a boil over high heat. Add the fettuccine and cook, stirring occasionally, until barely tender. Drain and return to the warm pot. Toss with the sauce and parsley. Transfer the pasta to a warmed large serving bowl. Serve immediately.

Spaghetti with Shrimp, Anchovies, and Bread Crumbs

Some Italian cooks avoid using cheese in seafood recipes, and often use sautéed bread crumbs instead.

1 cup fresh Italian or French bread crumbs, including crusts

1 pound spaghetti

¼ cup extra virgin olive oil, plus more for serving

¼ teaspoon salt

½ teaspoon crushed red pepper

6 anchovy fillets packed in oil, drained and minced

3 garlic cloves, minced

3 tablespoons chopped fresh parsley

2 teaspoons dried oregano

1 pound medium shrimp, peeled and deveined

MAKES 4 TO 6 SERVINGS

PREHEAT THE OVEN OR TOASTER OVEN TO 350° F. Spread the bread crumbs out on a baking sheet or on the toaster oven tray. Bake, stirring occasionally, until the crumbs are slightly dried and beginning to toast, 15 to 20 minutes in the oven, about 8 minutes in the toaster oven. Cool completely.

BRING A LARGE POT OF LIGHTLY SALTED WATER to a boil over high heat. Add the spaghetti and cook, stirring occasionally, until barely tender.

WHILE THE SPAGHETTI IS COOKING, heat 2 tablespoons of the oil in a large (12-inch) nonstick skillet over medium-high heat. Add the crumbs, salt, and red pepper. Cook, stirring often, until they turn golden brown, about 3 minutes. Transfer to a plate and set aside.

HEAT THE REMAINING 2 TABLESPOONS OIL in the skillet over medium heat. Add the anchovies, garlic, parsley, and oregano and stir until the anchovies dissolve into a paste, about 1 minute. Add the shrimp and cook, stirring occasionally, until pink and firm, 2 to 3 minutes.

DRAIN THE SPAGHETTI AND RETURN TO THE POT. Add the shrimp mixture and bread crumbs and toss well. Transfer to a warmed large serving bowl. Serve immediately, with a cruet of olive oil for adding to taste.

Fettuccine with Shrimp, Asparagus, and Mint

When asparagus is in season, I have to keep myself from making this quick pasta dish for dinner every night. For an extra-special first course for a company dinner, substitute fresh chives for the mint, and drizzle each serving with a few drops of white truffle oil.

BRING A LARGE POT OF LIGHTLY SALTED WATER to a boil over high heat. Add the asparagus and cook until crisp-tender, 2 to 3 minutes. Using a skimmer, transfer the asparagus to a bowl and set aside. (Do not rinse the asparagus under cold water.) Keep the water boiling.

ADD THE FETTUCCINE TO THE BOILING WATER and cook, stirring occasionally, until barely tender. During the last 30 seconds of cooking time, return the asparagus to the water to reheat.

WHEN THE FETTUCCINE IS ALMOST DONE, heat the butter in a large skillet over medium-high heat. Add the shrimp, shallots, and garlic. Cook, stirring occasionally, until the shrimps are pink and firm, 2 to 3 minutes. Remove from the heat and cover to keep warm.

SCOOP OUT AND RESERVE ½ cup of the pasta cooking water. Drain the fettuccine and asparagus and return to the pot. Add the shrimp mixture, Parmesan, salt, pepper, and mint. Toss, adding enough of the reserved pasta water to make a creamy sauce. Transfer to a warmed, large serving bowl. Serve immediately.

1 pound asparagus spears trimmed and cut into ½-inch lengths

1 pound fettuccine

2 tablespoons unsalted butter

1 pound medium shrimp, peeled and deveined

½ cup finely chopped shallots

1 garlic clove, minced

¾ cup freshly grated Parmesan cheese

¼ teaspoon salt

¼ teaspoon freshly ground pepper

2 tablespoons chopped fresh mint

MAKES 4 TO 6 SERVINGS

Spaghetti with Shrimp, Capers, and Garlic

This simple pasta can be whipped up in a hurry with pantry ingredients and shrimp, just the thing for a busy weeknight supper. Olive oil plays a big role here, so use extra virgin—a light oil won't do.

1 pound spaghetti

5 tablespoons extra virgin olive oil, plus more to taste

1½ pounds medium shrimp, peeled and deveined

3 tablespoons bottled capers, rinsed and coarsely chopped if large

3 cloves garlic, minced

3 tablespoons fresh lemon juice

3 tablespoons finely chopped fresh parsley

½ teaspoon salt

½ teaspoon freshly ground pepper

MAKES 4 TO 6 SERVINGS

BRING A LARGE POT OF LIGHTLY SALTED WATER to a boil over high heat. Add the spaghetti and cook, stirring occasionally, until barely tender.

WHILE THE PASTA IS COOKING, heat 2 tablespoons of the oil in a large (12-inch) skillet over medium heat. Add the shrimp and cook for 1 minute. Add the capers and garlic and cook, stirring occasionally, until the shrimps turn pink and firm, 2 to 3 minutes. Stir in the lemon juice and parsley and season with salt and pepper.

DRAIN THE SPAGHETTI, and return to the warmed pot. Add the shrimp and its sauce and toss, adding the remaining 3 tablespoons oil, or more, if you wish. Transfer to a warmed large serving bowl. Serve immediately.

Spaghetti with Shrimp in Garlicky Wine Sauce

Pasta with clam sauce is a classic dish, but I prefer to make a version with shrimp, because then there is no fussing with clam shells. Be careful when seasoning the finished dish—the clam juice can be quite salty.

PEEL AND DEVEIN THE SHRIMP, separately reserving the shells and shrimp. In a medium saucepan, bring the shrimp shells, clam juice, and wine to a simmer over medium heat. Simmer for 10 minutes. Strain the stock into a small bowl and set aside.

IN A LARGE (12-INCH) SKILLET, heat the oil over medium heat. Add the garlic, parsley, oregano, and red pepper. Cook, stirring constantly, until the garlic is fragrant, about 1 minute. Add the reserved stock and bring to a simmer. Add the shrimp and cook until pink and firm, 2 to 3 minutes.

MEANWHILE, BRING A LARGE POT OF LIGHTLY SALTED WATER to a boil over high heat. Add the spaghetti and cook, stirring occasionally, until barely tender. Drain and return to the pot. Add the shrimp sauce and butter and toss well. Season with salt. Transfer to a warmed large serving bowl. Serve immediately.

1 pound medium shrimp

1 cup bottled clam juice

1 cup dry white wine

2 tablespoons extra virgin olive oil

3 garlic cloves, minced

3 tablespoons chopped fresh parsley

1 teaspoon dried oregano

½ teaspoon crushed red pepper

1 pound spaghetti

2 tablespoons unsalted butter

Salt, to taste

MAKES 4 TO 6 SERVINGS

2 tablespoons extra virgin olive oil

1 large onion, cut into ¼-inch-thick
  half-moons

2 garlic cloves, minced

2 medium red bell peppers, seeded and
  cut into ½-inch-wide strips

2 medium Italian frying peppers, seeded
  and cut into ½-inch-wide strips

½ teaspoon salt

¼ teaspoon crushed red pepper

2 tablespoons balsamic vinegar

1 pound medium shrimp, peeled,
  deveined, and cut lengthwise in half

1 pound fettuccine

MAKES 4 TO 6 SERVINGS

Fettuccine with Shrimp, Pan-Roasted Peppers, and Balsamic Vinegar

In my neighborhood, pale green Italian frying peppers, often called cubanelles, are easy to find practically year-round, especially in late summer. If they are unavailable at your market, use green bell peppers, although they are slightly more bitter than the Italian ones.

IN A LARGE (12-INCH) NONSTICK SKILLET, heat the oil over medium heat. Add the onion and garlic and cover. Cook, stirring occasionally, until the onions are golden, about 5 minutes.

STIR IN THE BELL PEPPERS AND ITALIAN FRYING PEPPERS, salt, and red pepper. Cover and reduce the heat to medium-low. Cook, stirring occasionally, until the peppers are very tender, 20 to 25 minutes. Stir in the vinegar, then the shrimp. Cover and cook, stirring occasionally, until the shrimps are pink and firm, about 3 minutes.

MEANWHILE, BRING A LARGE POT OF LIGHTLY SALTED WATER to a boil over high heat. Add the fettuccine and cook, stirring occasionally until barely tender. Drain and return the pasta to the pot. Add the pepper and shrimp mixture and mix well. Transfer to a warmed large serving bowl. Serve immediately.

Spaghetti with Shrimp in Spicy Sicilian Sauce

When the mood strikes for a hearty, spicy sauce, choose this close relation to the popular *puttanesca*, made bold with anchovies, hot red pepper, and garlic.

BRING A LARGE POT OF LIGHTLY SALTED WATER to a boil over high heat. Add the spaghetti and cook, stirring occasionally, until barely tender.

WHILE THE PASTA IS COOKING, heat the olive oil and oil from the anchovy can in a large (12-inch) skillet over medium heat. Add the garlic and cook, stirring often, until golden, about 1 minute. Add the anchovy fillets and stir until they dissolve into paste, about 1 minute. Stir in the tomatoes, olives, capers, oregano, and red pepper and bring to a simmer. Reduce the heat to low and simmer for 5 minutes. Add the shrimp and cook, stirring occasionally, until the shrimps turn pink and firm, about 3 minutes.

DRAIN THE PASTA and return to the pot. Add the shrimp sauce and mix well. Transfer to a warmed, large serving bowl. Serve immediately.

1 pound spaghetti

1 tablespoon extra virgin olive oil

8 anchovy fillets packed in oil, oil reserved, drained and chopped

2 garlic cloves, minced

1 can (29 ounces) crushed tomatoes in puree

½ cup pitted and chopped Mediterranean black olives

2 tablespoons bottled capers, rinsed, and coarsely chopped if large

1 teaspoon dried oregano

½ teaspoon crushed red pepper

1 pound medium shrimp, peeled and deveined

MAKES 4 TO 6 SERVINGS

8 ounces medium shrimp, peeled and deveined

1 tablespoon fresh lemon juice

1 large egg, separated

¼ pound cream cheese, at room temperature

6 tablespoons fresh bread crumbs

2 tablespoons chopped fresh cilantro

1 teaspoon minced fresh ginger

¼ teaspoon salt

¼ teaspoon freshly ground white pepper

Dash of cayenne

36 round won ton or gyoza wrappers

GINGER SAUCE

2 tablespoons unsalted butter

¼ cup minced shallots

4 teaspoons minced fresh ginger

2 cups dry white wine

3 cups heavy cream

½ teaspoon salt

½ teaspoon freshly ground white pepper

1 tablespoon minced fresh cilantro

Fresh cilantro leaves, for garnish

**MAKES 6 FIRST-COURSE OR
4 MAIN-COURSE SERVINGS**

Shrimp Agnolotti in Ginger Sauce

This high-style recipe is based on one from Ocean Garden Products, shrimp purveyors to some of America's finest restaurants. It is a rich, elegant dish—I serve six agnolotti per person as a first course, but I have also served eight per person as a main course, topped with a few sautéed shrimp. Both the agnolotti and the sauce can be prepared well ahead of serving. Agnolotti are round Piedmont-style ravioli, and are usually stuffed with meat or cheese—shrimp is a wonderful change. Of course, in Italy, they would be made with handmade pasta, but store-bought won-ton wrappers are a good substitute. When choosing the wrappers, try to buy a brand without preservatives.

TO MAKE THE AGNOLOTTI, in a food processor, pulse the shrimp, lemon juice, and egg yolk until finely chopped. Do not puree. Transfer to a medium bowl. Add the cream cheese, bread crumbs, cilantro, ginger, salt, pepper, and cayenne. Mash with a rubber spatula until well combined.

IN A SMALL BOWL, beat the egg white with 1 teaspoon water until foamy. Using a pastry brush, brush the edges of 1 won ton wrapper with the egg white mixture. Place a rounded teaspoon of the shrimp mixture in the center of the wrapper. Top with another wrapper, pressing the edges to seal. Place on a kitchen towel–lined baking sheet. Repeat with the remaining wrappers and filling. Cover loosely with plastic wrap and refrigerate until ready to cook, up to 4 hours.

TO MAKE THE SAUCE, in a large, heavy-bottomed saucepan, heat the butter over medium heat. Add the shallots and ginger. Cook, stirring often, until the shallots are softened, about 2 minutes. Add the wine and bring to a boil over high heat. Cook until the wine is reduced to a glaze, about 10 minutes. Add the cream and boil until reduced to about 2¼ cups, about 7 minutes. Season with the salt and pepper. Keep the sauce warm. (The sauce can be prepared up to 2 hours ahead and kept at room temperature with a piece of plastic wrap pressed directly on the sauce's surface to keep a skin from forming. Reheat gently over low heat.)

WHEN READY TO SERVE, bring a large pot of lightly salted water to a boil over high heat. Add the agnolotti and cook until tender, 3 to 4 minutes. Remove from the heat, pour in 1 cup of cold water to stop the cooking, and let the agnolotti stand in the hot water while preparing the plates.

STRAIN THE SAUCE INTO A WARMED BOWL, pressing hard on the solids. Spoon a scant ¼ cup sauce in the center of each of 4 to 6 dinner plates. Using a skimmer, remove the agnolotti from the hot water and arrange six (for an appetizer) or eight (for a main course) on top of the sauce. Drizzle any remaining sauce on the agnolotti. Serve immediately, garnished with cilantro leaves.

SHRIMP AGNOLOTTI IN CORIANDER BROTH:
For a lighter alternative, serve the agnolotti in Shrimp Stock with Coriander (page 17) instead of the ginger sauce. Cook the agnolotti in boiling salted water just before serving. Place the agnolotti in warmed serving bowls, and add ½ cup hot broth per serving. Garnish with peeled and seeded ripe plum tomatoes and whole cilantro leaves and serve immediately.

Spaghetti with Shrimp, Zucchini, and Prosciutto

2 tablespoons extra virgin olive oil

3 ounces prosciutto, sliced ¼-inch thick, finely chopped

1 pound medium shrimp, peeled and deveined

2 large zucchini, cut into ½-inch dice

2 garlic cloves, minced

2 tablespoons finely chopped fresh sage or 1 teaspoon dried sage

½ teaspoon salt

¼ teaspoon freshly ground pepper

1 pound spaghetti

½ cup freshly grated Parmesan cheese, plus more for serving

MAKES 4 TO 6 SERVINGS

Sautéed zucchini slices are delicious, served as a side dish or turned into a great pasta sauce studded with shrimp. The trick to getting them flecked with golden brown spots is not to salt the zucchini during cooking, or the rendered juices will inhibit browning. Sage doesn't show up in many pasta sauces, but it is a pleasant surprise here.

IN A LARGE (12-INCH) NONSTICK SKILLET, heat 1 tablespoon of the oil over medium heat. Add the prosciutto and cook, stirring occasionally, until lightly browned, about 3 minutes. Add the shrimp and cook, stirring occasionally, until pink and firm, 2 to 3 minutes. Transfer to a bowl and cover to keep warm.

ADD THE REMAINING 1 TABLESPOON OIL to the skillet and heat over medium-high heat. Add the zucchini and cook, stirring occasionally, until golden brown, about 8 minutes. Add the garlic, sage, salt, and pepper and stir until the garlic is fragrant, about 1 minute.

MEANWHILE, BRING A LARGE POT OF LIGHTLY SALTED WATER to a boil over high heat. Add the spaghetti and cook, stirring occasionally, until barely tender. Scoop out and reserve ½ cup of the pasta cooking water. Drain the spaghetti and return to the pot. Stir in the zucchini and shrimp mixtures and the Parmesan. Mix well, gradually adding enough of the pasta water to make a creamy sauce. Transfer to a warmed, large serving bowl. Serve immediately.

Indonesian Fried Noodles with Shrimp and Ham

Pancit, the national noodle dish of Indonesia, is one of those dishes that can be simple or elaborate. There are other versions with chicken and Chinese sausage (which can be added, of course), but this less complicated variation is delicious.

BRING A LARGE SAUCEPAN OF LIGHTLY SALTED WATER to a boil over high heat. Add the shrimp and cook until pink and firm, about 3 minutes. Using a slotted skimmer, remove the shrimps from the water, transfer to a colander, and rinse under cold water until cool enough to handle. Peel the shrimps, discarding the shells, and set aside.

RETURN THE SHRIMP COOKING WATER TO A BOIL over high heat. Add the egg noodles and cook until barely tender, 2 to 4 minutes. Do not overcook. Drain, rinse under cold running water, and toss with 1 tablespoon of the oil.

HEAT 2 TABLESPOONS OIL IN A LARGE (12-INCH) NONSTICK SKILLET over medium heat. Add the onion and garlic and cook, stirring often, until the onion is softened but not browned, about 3 minutes. Stir in the ham, carrots, and celery and cook, stirring often, until the celery is crisp-tender, about 2 minutes. Stir in the paprika and pepper, then the fish sauce. Transfer to a bowl, add the shrimps, and cover with foil to keep warm. Wipe out the skillet with a paper towel.

ADD THE REMAINING 2 TABLESPOONS OIL to the skillet and heat over medium-high heat. Add the noodles and cook, stirring occasionally, until heated through. Transfer the fried noodles to a platter and top with the shrimp sauce. Sprinkle with the chopped scallions. Serve immediately, accompanied by the lime wedges.

1 pound medium shrimp

1 pound fresh Chinese egg noodles, or fresh linguine

5 tablespoons vegetable oil

1 medium onion, chopped

1 garlic clove, minced

8 ounces boiled ham, sliced ¼ inch thick and cut into ¼-inch-wide strips

2 medium carrots, cut into ⅛-inch-wide matchsticks

2 medium celery ribs, cut on the diagonal into ⅛-inch-thick slices

1 teaspoon sweet Hungarian paprika

¼ teaspoon freshly ground pepper

2 tablespoons Indonesian fish sauce (pastis, see page 37)

Chopped scallions, for garnish

Lime wedges, for garnish

MAKES 4 TO 6 SERVINGS

Moroccan-Spiced Shrimp on Fruited Couscous

Couscous, tiny semolina pasta, is becoming more and more popular with cooks who are cooking against the clock—it cooks in five minutes. Here's a sweet-and-spicy shrimp and vegetable stir-fry to serve on top of couscous.

IN A LARGE (12-INCH) NONSTICK SKILLET, heat the oil over medium-high heat. Add the onion and carrots. Stir until the onion is golden about 5 minutes. Add the zucchini and cook until almost tender, about 4 minutes. Add the garlic, paprika, cumin, coriander, cayenne, salt, and saffron and stir for 30 seconds. Add the tomatoes, lemon juice, and sugar and stir for 1 minute. Add the stock and bring to a simmer. Cook until slightly reduced, about 2 minutes.

ADD THE SHRIMP AND COVER. Cook until the shrimps are pink and firm, 2 to 3 minutes. Serve immediately, spooned over the couscous.

Fruited Couscous

In a medium saucepan, bring 1 cup fresh orange juice, 1 cup water, ½ cup raisins, and ½ teaspoon salt to a boil over high heat. Stir in 1 box (10 ounces) quick-cooking couscous (1½ cups). Remove from the heat and cover tightly. Let stand for 5 minutes or until the couscous absorbs the liquid. Fluff with a fork and serve immediately.

2 tablespoons extra virgin olive oil

1 medium onion, chopped

2 medium carrots, cut into ¼-inch-thick rounds

2 medium zucchini, cut into ½-inch cubes

2 garlic cloves, minced

1 teaspoon sweet Hungarian paprika

1 teaspoon ground cumin

½ teaspoon ground coriander

¼ teaspoon cayenne

¼ teaspoon salt

⅛ teaspoon crushed saffron threads

1 can (16 ounces) plum tomatoes, drained and chopped

2 tablespoons fresh lemon juice

1 teaspoon sugar

1 cup Shrimp Stock (page 16) or chicken broth

1 pound medium shrimp, peeled and deveined

Fruited Couscous (recipe follows)

MAKES 4 TO 6 SERVINGS

1 pound medium shrimp

6 ounces thin rice noodles, also called rice vermicelli or *mai fun* (available in Asian markets and many supermarkets)

3 tablespoons soy sauce

1 tablespoon Madras-style curry powder

1 tablespoon light brown sugar

¼ teaspoon salt

2 tablespoons vegetable oil

1 tablespoon minced fresh ginger

1 garlic clove, minced

1 small onion, cut into ⅛-inch-thick half-moons

2 medium celery ribs, cut on the diagonal into ⅛-inch-thick slices

1 small red bell pepper, seeded and cut into ¼-inch-wide strips

4 ounces snow peas, trimmed, strings removed, and cut on the diagonal into ¼-inch-wide strips

Lime wedges, for serving

MAKES 4 TO 6 SERVINGS

Curried Rice Noodles with Shrimp

This dish is a specialty of Singapore, whose merchants traded with Indian ships and learned to love the spicy curry flavor.

PEEL AND DEVEIN THE SHRIMP, separately reserving the shells and shrimps. In a small saucepan, bring the shrimp shells with enough cold water to cover to a simmer over medium heat. Reduce the heat to low and simmer for 15 minutes. Strain into a small bowl and set aside.

MEANWHILE, PLACE THE RICE NOODLES in a large bowl and add enough hot water to cover. Let stand just until softened and supple, about 10 minutes. Drain and cover with a moist kitchen towel to keep the noodles from drying out. Set aside.

IN A SMALL BOWL, mix ½ cup of the reserved broth (reserving the remaining broth) with the soy sauce, curry powder, brown sugar, and salt. Set aside.

HEAT A LARGE (12-INCH) NONSTICK SKILLET over medium-high heat. Add 1 tablespoon of the oil, swirling the skillet to coat with oil, and heat until the oil is very hot. Add the shrimps and stir-fry until pink and firm, about 2 minutes. Remove to a plate and set aside.

ADD THE REMAINING 1 TABLESPOON OIL TO THE SKILLET, swirl to coat, and heat until the oil is very hot. Add the ginger and garlic and stir-fry until fragrant, 15 to 30 seconds. Add the onion, celery, bell pepper and stir-fry just until the vegetables are crisp-tender, about 3 minutes. Add the snow peas and stir-fry for 1 minute. Stir in the soy sauce mixture, then add the drained noodles and reserved shrimp. Stir-fry until the noodles are heated through and coated with the sauce. (If the noodles seem dry, add some of the remaining shrimp broth to moisten.) Serve immediately.

Southeast Asian Basil Shrimp with Rice Sticks

Southeast Asian rice noodles are often labeled "rice sticks." Look for medium-wide noodles called *pho* (not the thin ones, sometimes called *vermicelli*). These noodles are not boiled, just briefly soaked in hot water until supple—don't oversoak them, or they will break up when stir-fried.

PEEL AND DEVEIN THE SHRIMP, separately reserving the shells and shrimps. In a medium saucepan, bring the shrimp shells with enough cold water to cover to a simmer over medium heat. Reduce the heat to low and simmer for 15 minutes. Strain into a small bowl and set aside ½ cup of the shrimp broth.

MEANWHILE, PLACE THE RICE STICKS IN A LARGE BOWL and add enough hot water to cover. Let stand just until softened and supple, 10 to 15 minutes. Drain and cover with a moist kitchen towel to keep the rice sticks from drying out.

MEANWHILE, HEAT A LARGE (12-INCH) SKILLET over medium-high heat. Add the oil, swirling the skillet to coat, and heat until the oil is very hot. Add the mushrooms and bell pepper. Cook, stirring often, until the mushrooms are lightly browned, about 8 minutes. Add the shallots, garlic, ginger, and chile rounds and stir-fry for 1 minute. Stir in the reserved shrimp broth, the fish sauce, and ¼ cup water and bring to a boil.

STIR IN THE SHRIMPS AND THE BASIL. Cook, stirring constantly, for 1 minute. Add the drained rice sticks and stir gently until they have absorbed some of the liquid and the shrimps are pink and firm, about 1 minute more. Serve immediately.

1½ pounds medium shrimp

8 ounces medium rice sticks (*pho*)

2 tablespoons vegetable oil

10 ounces white mushrooms, cut into quarters

1 large red bell pepper, seeded and cut into ⅛-inch-wide strips

⅓ cup chopped shallots

2 large garlic cloves, minced

1 tablespoon grated fresh ginger (use the large holes on a box grater)

1 tablespoon thinly sliced chile rounds, from 2 small Thai chiles or 1 medium jalapeño

¼ cup Asian fish sauce (see page 37)

1 cup (packed) holy basil or regular basil leaves, coarsely shredded

MAKES 4 SERVINGS

Risotto Primavera with Shrimp

In Italy, risotto is served always as a first course to a elegant meal, but it is quite rich, and may be served as an entrée. Arborio rice is the most widely available Italian rice (only Italian rice is starchy enough to make a proper risotto); the less familiar Carnaroli and Vialone Nano varieties create a risotto with firmer grains and a creamier sauce. With risotto, texture is all-important. Be flexible with the cooking time, adjusting it as needed to cook rice just until al dente.

PEEL AND DEVEIN THE SHRIMP, separately reserving the shells and shrimps. In a large saucepan, bring the shrimp shells, chicken broth, and 4 cups water to a simmer over medium heat. Reduce the heat to low and simmer for 30 minutes. Strain into a bowl, then return the broth to the pot and keep at a bare simmer over very low heat.

IN A LARGE, HEAVY-BOTTOMED POT, heat 1 tablespoon of the oil over medium heat. Add the shrimps and cook, stirring occasionally, until barely firm and opaque, 1 to 2 minutes. Transfer to a plate and set aside.

ADD THE REMAINING 2 TABLESPOONS OIL to the pot and heat. Add the shallots, carrot, and celery and cook, stirring often, until softened, about 2 minutes. Add the rice and cook, stirring often, until it turns translucent, 2 to 3 minutes. Pour in the wine and cook, stirring almost constantly, until the rice absorbs the wine. Ladle in enough of the simmering broth to barely reach the top of the rice (the exact amount depends on the size of the pot, but it is usually around 1 cup). Reduce

(CONTINUED)

1 pound medium shrimp

3½ cups chicken broth, preferably home-made, or use low-sodium canned broth

3 tablespoons extra virgin olive oil

⅓ cup minced shallots

1 small carrot, cut into ¼-inch dice

1 medium celery rib, cut into ¼-inch dice

1 pound Italian rice for risotto, such as Arborio, Carnaroli, or Vialone

1 cup dry white wine

1 cup thawed frozen peas

½ cup freshly grated Parmesan cheese

2 tablespoons unsalted butter

2 tablespoons chopped fresh parsley

½ teaspoon salt

¼ teaspoon freshly ground pepper

MAKES 4 TO 6 SERVINGS

the heat to low and stir for about 3 minutes, or until the rice absorbs the stock, adjusting the heat as necessary to keep the risotto at a simmer. Ladle another cup of broth into the pot and stir until the rice absorbs the broth. Repeat the procedure, stirring the hot broth into the rice, until the rice is almost tender, 20 to 30 minutes. You may have some stock leftover; if all the stock is used before the rice is tender, switch to hot water. During the last 2 minutes of cooking, stir in the shrimps and peas. When the rice is just tender, stir in a final cup of stock to give the risotto a spoonable, loose consistency.

STIR IN THE PARMESAN, BUTTER, SALT, AND PEPPER. Serve immediately, in warmed wide soup bowls.

Shrimp Jambalaya

I had tried many recipes for jambalaya, but most of them, no matter how tasty, ended up with an impossible-to-clean pot with rice burned on the bottom. Then, during a trip to Cajun country, a cook showed me the foolproof way to make jambalaya by simmering a pot of spicy tomato sauce and folding it into cooked rice.

IN A MEDIUM SAUCEPAN, heat the oil over medium heat. Add the ham, scallions, bell pepper, and celery. Cook, stirring occasionally, until the vegetables soften, about 4 minutes. Stir in the Cajun Seasoning and garlic. Stir in the tomatoes and bring to a simmer. Reduce the heat to medium-low and simmer until slightly thickened, about 25 minutes. Add the shrimp and cook until pink and firm, 2 to 3 minutes.

MEANWHILE, IN ANOTHER HEAVY SAUCEPAN, bring the stock, rice, and salt to a boil over high heat. Reduce the heat to low and cover tightly. Cook until the rice absorbs the stock and is tender, about 15 minutes. Remove from the heat and let stand, covered, for 5 minutes.

IN A LARGE SERVING BOWL, combine the rice and tomato sauce. Sprinkle with the scallions and serve immediately.

1 tablespoon vegetable oil

6 ounces smoked ham, cut into ½-inch cubes

1 cup chopped scallions, white and green parts

1 small red bell pepper, seeded and chopped

1 large celery rib with leaves, chopped

1 tablespoon Cajun Seasoning (page 71)

2 garlic cloves, minced

1 can (35 ounces) tomatoes in thick puree, pulsed in a food processor until coarsely chopped

1 pound medium shrimp, peeled (use the shells in the stock) and deveined

3 cups Shrimp Stock (page 16)

1½ cups long-grain rice

½ teaspoon salt

Chopped scallions, for garnish

MAKES 4 SERVINGS

¾ pound green beans, trimmed and cut into ½-inch pieces

6 ounces bacon, chopped

1 medium onion, chopped

1½ cups long-grain rice

3 cups Shrimp Stock (page 16)

¾ teaspoon salt

¼ teaspoon crushed red pepper

1 pound medium shrimp, peeled (use the shells in the stock) and deveined

2 tablespoons chopped fresh parsley

MAKES 4 SERVINGS

Shrimp and Green Bean Pilau

Pilau is a popular dish in the Carolinas, and deserves to be better known in the other states. This recipe adds green beans to make it a substantial one-pot meal.

BRING A MEDIUM SAUCEPAN OF LIGHTLY SALTED WATER to a boil over high heat. Add the green beans and cook just until crisp-tender, about 2 minutes. Drain and rinse under cold water. Set aside. Wipe the saucepan dry.

IN THE SAME SAUCEPAN, cook the bacon over medium heat until crisp and brown, about 5 minutes. Using a slotted spoon, transfer the bacon to paper towels. Set aside.

POUR OFF ALL BUT 2 TABLESPOONS OF THE BACON FAT. Add the onion to the fat and cook, stirring occasionally, until softened, about 3 minutes. Add the rice and stir for 1 minute. Pour in the stock, salt, and red pepper and bring to a boil. Reduce the heat to low and cover tightly. Cook until the rice is tender, about 15 minutes.

REMOVE THE SAUCEPAN FROM THE HEAT. Fluff the rice with a fork and stir in the reserved bacon and green beans and the shrimp. Cover tightly and let stand until the shrimps turn pink and firm (the heat from the rice will cook them), about 10 minutes. Serve immediately, sprinkled with the parsley.

Malaysian Fried Rice

The Malaysian version of the classic fried rice uses a savory puree to season the dish, and it is served with a variety of garnishes to give it a balance of hot and cold temperatures with crisp and soft textures. You can use 4 cups of leftover rice, of course, but the proportions here are for starting from scratch. Just be sure the rice is well chilled, or you will end up with fried rice mush.

IN A MEDIUM SAUCEPAN, bring the rice, salt, and 2⅔ cups water to a boil over high heat. Reduce the heat to low and cover. Cook until the rice is tender, about 15 minutes. Remove from the heat and let stand, covered, for 5 minutes. Transfer to a bowl and cool to room temperature. Cover and refrigerate until chilled, at least 2 hours. Measure out 4 cups of rice.

IN A FOOD PROCESSOR, process the onion, bell pepper, jalapeño, garlic, and shrimp paste until pureed.

IN A LARGE (12-INCH) NONSTICK SKILLET, heat the oil over medium heat. Add the onion puree and cook, stirring often, until the liquid evaporates and the mixture looks somewhat drier, about 2 minutes. Add the shrimp and cook, stirring often, just until the shrimps turn opaque, about 1 minute. Add the rice and scallions and stir for 1 minute. Sprinkle with the soy sauce and continue stirring until the rice is evenly colored and heated through, about 1 minute more. Transfer to a serving platter, garnish with the cucumber and tomato and serve immediately.

NOTE: Fine shrimp sauce is a pungent salty seasoning sold in jars in Asian markets. Do not confuse it with dried shrimp paste, sold in blocks. Anchovy paste is a very good substitute.

1⅓ cups long-grain rice

½ teaspoon salt

1 medium onion, quartered

1 small red bell pepper, seeded and chopped

2 jalapeños, seeded and chopped

2 garlic cloves, crushed

½ teaspoon fine shrimp sauce or 1 teaspoon anchovy paste (see Note)

2 tablespoons vegetable oil

1½ pounds medium shrimp, peeled and deveined

4 scallions, white and green parts, trimmed and chopped

2 tablespoons soy sauce

1 medium cucumber, peeled, seeded, and thinly sliced

1 medium tomato, cut into wedges

MAKES 4 TO 6 SERVINGS

Shrimp from the Grill

**GRILLED SHRIMP, SAGE,
AND PANCETTA SPEDINI**

Shrimp on the Grill

Sizzling shrimp, hot off the grill, is a pleasure that is no longer limited to the summer months. More and more cooks are grilling year-round on gas grills. Even though I prefer the taste of charcoal-grilled food, I admit that the convenience of a gas grill is hard to overlook. Whether you cook your shrimp over charcoal or gas, do not overcook it! Remove shrimp from the grill as soon as it turns opaque and firm, four to six minutes, depending on the size of the shrimp. Here are some considerations before tossing the shrimp on the barbecue.

SHRIMP SIZE: This is one case where bigger is better. Colossal (under 15 shrimp per pound) and jumbo (under 20 per pound) are best because their size makes it easier to gauge doneness. But such huge shrimp are pricey. Extra-large and large shrimp (21 to 30 shrimp per pound) can be fine, as long as the shrimps are watched carefully and removed from the grill as soon as they are firm and cooked.

MARINATING: The purpose of marinating shrimp is to add flavor. Many marinades have acidic ingredients like citrus juice or wine. If allowed to remain in contact with the delicate shrimp flesh for longer than two hours, the acids will "cook" the shrimp, turning it opaque and firm, like seviche, the Mexican marinated seafood dish. Overmarinated shrimp has a mushy, unpleasant texture after grilling. Unpeeled shrimp can be marinated for no longer than 2 hours. Peeled shrimp can also be marinated that long, but it usually absorbs enough flavor in 15 to 30 minutes. To discourage bacterial growth, always marinate in the refrigerator, not at room temperature.

Acidic ingredients in the marinade can also react with the holding utensil. Heavy-duty self-sealing bags (especially the large freezer size) are your best choice. They are efficient and take up less space in the refrigerator. Otherwise, always marinate in a bowl or baking dish made of a nonreactive material, such as glass, ceramic, stainless steel, or enameled cast iron—not an aluminum or unlined cast iron pot.

The marinades in this chapter are on the thick side, so they stick to the shrimp instead of draining away. Some of them are so thick that they form a glaze when the shrimps are grilled. There is no reason for basting the shrimps with any remaining marinade left in the bowl, since they cook so quickly, but if you can't resist, go ahead and baste.

PEELED VERSUS UNPEELED: To peel or not to peel. That is the question. Like so many other big questions in life, it is a matter of personal taste.

The flesh of unpeeled shrimp is obviously protected by the shell, which helps hold in juices. It is fun to eat shell-on shrimp, licking your fingers to get every last drop of marinade. Unpeeled shrimp is best with highly seasoned marinades, such as Thai Lemongrass and Chile Marinade or Tandoori Marinade.

Peeled shrimp is easier to eat at the table, and soaks up the flavors of marinades and glazes more readily. Always marinate peeled shrimp to add moisture. If you are in a hurry and don't have time to mix up a marinade, give the shrimp a ten-minute soak in a splash of extra virgin olive oil, salt, and pepper (and a bit if minced garlic, if you like).

HEAT LEVEL: Shrimp is delicate and easy to overcook. It is not like steak, where the ideal is a crisp, browned exterior. If shrimp is cooked over extremely high heat, it will dry out. (An exception is peeled colossal shrimp wrapped in bacon—the bacon protects the shrimp, and cooking over high heat crisps the bacon.) Use medium-high heat to grill shrimp. With a gas grill it's easy—just turn the thermostat dial to Medium. With charcoal, it's a matter of letting the fire burn down until moderately, not blazing, hot. Let the fire burn until the coals are covered with white ash, 25 to 30 minutes (less if you use a chimney starter). Hold your hand over the coals just above the level of the cooking rack. If you can count to three before you have to pull your hand away, the fire is medium-hot, just right for shrimp. If the fire is too hot, just let it burn down a few more minutes.

Always oil the cooking rack so the shrimps don't stick. Also, cover your grill while cooking—it helps to contain the heat that would otherwise escape, turning the grill into an oven.

BROILING VERSUS GRILLING: All of the dishes in this chapter can be done in the broiler. Adjust the rack about six inches from the source of heat and preheat the broiler. Place the drained marinated shrimps in a lightly oiled broiling ban. Broil until the tops turn pink, then turn over and continue broiling until the shrimps are opaque and firm. The exact broiling time depends on the size of the shrimp—about three to four minutes for large shrimp, five to seven minutes for colossal shrimp.

What, No Shrimp Kebabs? I myself am not a fan of shrimp and vegetable kebabs. I like to concentrate on cooking the shrimp to perfection and not worry about how the vegetables next to the shrimp are doing. Invariably, when the shrimp is just right, the

(CONTINUED)

zucchini is still raw. So let the shrimp fly solo and grill accompanying vegetables separately.

On the other hand, threading shrimps onto skewers makes them easier to turn and keeps them from falling through the rack onto the coals. Bamboo skewers are convenient and inexpensive. Before use, soak the skewers in cold water to cover for 30 minutes, then drain (unsoaked skewers will burn over the coals). Shrimps threaded onto a single skewer will twirl when you try to flip them from one side to the other. To solve this problem, threat the shrimps onto two soaked bamboo skewers held slightly apart and parallel to each other. Pierce each shrimp through the top and bottom while threading so it keeps its natural curve. Don't crowd shrimps onto the skewer, or they will take longer to cook.

Basic Grilled Shrimp

Hardwood lump charcoal may give the best flavor, but it burns very hot—let it burn down sufficiently before adding the shrimp. High-quality charcoal briquettes heat more evenly. If you want more wood flavor, sprinkle soaked and drained wooden chips over the coals before grilling the shrimp.

2 pounds large, extra-large, jumbo, or colossal shrimp

Marinade (pages 130, 131)

Bamboo skewers, soaked for 30 minutes in water and drained (optional)

MAKES 4 SERVINGS

IN A LARGE, HEAVY-DUTY, SELF-SEALING PLASTIC BAG, combine the shrimp and the marinade. Refrigerate, turning the shrimp occasionally, for at least 15 minutes and up to 2 hours for peeled shrimp, at least 1 hour and up to 2 hours for unpeeled shrimp.

FOR LARGE OR EXTRA-LARGE SHRIMP, build a charcoal fire in an out-door grill and let it burn until the coals are covered with white ash and you can hold your hand at rack level for about 3 seconds (medium-hot). If using a gas grill, preheat to Medium. For jumbo or colossal shrimp, build a very hot fire that you can hold your hand over for only 1 to 2 seconds, or preheat a gas grill to High. Lightly oil the rack.

DRAIN THE SHRIMP. If desired, skewer the shrimps on the bamboo skewers as described on page 128. Cover the grill and cook until the shrimps begin to turn opaque around the edges. Turn and continue grilling just until pink and firm. The total cooking time depends on the size of the shrimp: 3 to 4 minutes for large and extra-large shrimp, 5 to 7 minutes for jumbo and colossal shrimp. Remove the shrimps from the skewers, if using, and serve immediately.

½ cup dry white wine

⅓ cup extra virgin olive oil

Grated zest of 1 lemon

3 tablespoons fresh lemon juice

2 garlic cloves, crushed through a press

2 tablespoons chopped fresh parsley

2 tablespoons chopped fresh basil or
 1½ teaspoons dried basil

2 teaspoons chopped fresh thyme or
 ½ teaspoon dried thyme

2 teaspoons chopped fresh rosemary
 or ½ teaspoon dried rosemary

½ teaspoon fennel seeds, crushed

¼ teaspoon salt

¼ teaspoon crushed red pepper

**MAKES ABOUT 1¼ CUPS, ENOUGH
FOR 2 POUNDS SHRIMP**

White Wine and Herb Marinade

Herbs from a summer garden will make this simple
marinade extraordinary.

IN A MEDIUM NONREACTIVE BOWL, mix all of the ingredients. Use as a
marinade for shrimp, following the instructions on page 129.

Honey-Mustard Marinade

Make this sweet and tangy marinade with a full-flavored honey, such as sage or chestnut.

IN A MEDIUM NONREACTIVE BOWL, mix all of the ingredients. Use as a marinade for shrimp, following the instructions on page 129.

1 cup Dijon mustard

⅓ cup plus 1 tablespoon honey

2 tablespoons vegetable oil

2 tablespoons soy sauce

2 tablespoons finely chopped chives or scallions

1 tablespoon finely chopped fresh tarragon or 2 teaspoons dried tarragon

½ teaspoon freshly ground pepper

MAKES ABOUT 1½ CUPS, ENOUGH FOR 2 POUNDS SHRIMP

Chipotle-Pineapple Glaze

Sweet and hot make a sensational flavor combination. This glaze works best on peeled shrimp.

1 cup (12-ounce jar) pineapple preserves

3 tablespoons fresh lime juice

2 teaspoons finely chopped chipotle peppers en adobo (see page 68)

2 garlic cloves, minced

¼ teaspoon salt

2 tablespoons vegetable oil

MAKES ABOUT 1¼ CUPS, ENOUGH FOR 2 POUNDS SHRIMP

IN A SMALL SAUCEPAN, bring all of the ingredients except the oil to a simmer over medium heat, stirring constantly. Transfer to a bowl and cool completely. Whisk in the oil. Use as a marinade for shrimp, following the instructions on page 129.

Jerked Shrimp Rub

In Jamaica, jerk is a spicy seasoning paste for grilled foods. For real Jamaican flavor, use a Scotch bonnet pepper, but be forewarned—it is much hotter than jalapeños or other familiar chiles, and a little goes a long way. If you have tender skin, be sure to protect your hands with rubber gloves when chopping the chile or handling the paste.

IN A BLENDER, process all of the ingredients until they form a paste. Use as a marinade for shrimp, rubbing the mixture well into the shrimps through the plastic bag. Grill following the instructions on page 129.

6 scallions, white and green parts, coarsely chopped

2 teaspoons seeded and minced Scotch bonnet chile pepper or 1 jalapeño

4 garlic cloves, minced

¼ cup vegetable oil

¼ cup fresh lime juice

2 tablespoons soy sauce

2 teaspoons dried thyme

1 teaspoon ground allspice

MAKES ABOUT 1¼ CUPS, ENOUGH FOR 2 POUNDS SHRIMP

1 cup plain lowfat yogurt
1 small onion, coarsely chopped
2 garlic cloves, crushed under a knife
1 tablespoon minced fresh ginger
1½ teaspoons ground coriander
1½ teaspoons ground cumin
1 teaspoon hot paprika or sweet paprika
¼ teaspoon turmeric
¼ teaspoon ground cardamom
⅛ teaspoon ground cinnamon
⅛ teaspoon cayenne

MAKES ABOUT 1⅓ CUPS, ENOUGH FOR 2 POUNDS SHRIMP

Tandoori Marinade

A yogurt-based marinade gives grilled foods a wonderful tang and beautiful glaze. Indian cooks would prepare these marinated shrimp in a barrel-shaped clay tandoori oven, but grilling them over coals gives excellent results.

IN A BLENDER OR A FOOD PROCESSOR fitted with the metal blade, process all of the ingredients into a puree. Use as a marinade for shrimp, following the instructions on page 129.

Grated zest of 1 sour or Valencia orange

½ cup fresh sour orange juice or ¼ cup
fresh Valencia orange juice and ¼ cup
fresh lemon juice

3 tablespoons extra virgin olive oil

2 teaspoons dried oregano

4 garlic cloves, crushed through a press

¼ teaspoon salt

¼ teaspoon hot pepper sauce, preferably
Caribbean-style with Scotch bonnet
chiles, or to taste

**MAKES ABOUT 1¼ CUPS, ENOUGH
FOR 2 POUNDS SHRIMP**

Caribbean Sour Orange Marinade

Sour oranges, available in Hispanic markets, are much different from the familiar sweet oranges. They have a very sour juice that makes a great marinade. If you can't find sour oranges, mix equal amounts of orange and lemon juice.

IN A MEDIUM NONREACTIVE BOWL, mix all of the ingredients. Use as a marinade for shrimp. Do not marinate for longer than 30 minutes, or the marinade will change the texture of the shrimp. Grill, following the instructions on page 129.

Indonesian Curry Marinade

When a can of unshaken coconut milk is opened, the milk is in two layers: a thick top layer of coconut cream, with thinner milk underneath. Spoon the thick coconut cream from the top to use in this spicy marinade.

IN A BLENDER, process all of the ingredients until pureed. Use as a marinade for shrimp, following the instructions on page 129.

¾ cup canned coconut cream

1 scallion, white and green parts, chopped

2 teaspoons minced fresh ginger

2 garlic cloves, chopped

2 tablespoons soy sauce

2 teaspoons light brown sugar

1½ teaspoons Madras-style curry powder

MAKES ABOUT 1¼ CUPS, ENOUGH FOR 2 POUNDS SHRIMP

Thai Lemongrass and Chile Marinade

Thai cooks would never peel shrimp before marinating—serve this with family or good friends who don't mind rolling up their sleeves and digging in.

4   lemongrass stalks

½   cup fresh lime juice

¼   cup Asian fish sauce (see page 37)

¼   cup vegetable oil

2   scallions, white and green parts, chopped

¼   cup chopped fresh cilantro, including stems

2   serranos or jalapeño chiles, seeded and chopped

Grated zest of 2 limes

6   garlic cloves, chopped

½   teaspoon crushed red pepper

MAKES ABOUT 1¾ CUPS, ENOUGH FOR 2 TO 3 POUNDS SHRIMP

REMOVE THE TOUGH OUTER LAYER OF THE LEMONGRASS. Using a sharp knife or a mini-food processor, mince the tender bottom 4 to 6 inches of the stalks. You should have about ½ cup. In a blender, combine the lemongrass with the remaining ingredients until they form a paste. Use as a marinade for shrimp, following the instructions on page 129.

Asian Smoky Tea Marinade

Laapsang souchong tea is a black tea with an unusual twist—the leaves have been smoked, giving the brewed tea a heady aroma. This tea is so full-bodied and rich, it can be used as the base for a contemporary teriyaki-style marinade.

IN A SMALL BOWL, steep the tea in the water for 10 minutes to make a strong brewed tea. Strain the tea into a medium bowl and cool completely. Add the soy sauce, hoisin sauce, rice wine, ginger, garlic, and chili paste and whisk until combined. Use as a marinade for shrimp, following the instructions on page 129.

2 tablespoons laapsang souchong tea leaves or 2 tea bags

1 cup boiling water

3 tablespoons soy sauce

2 tablespoons hoisin sauce

2 tablespoons rice wine or dry sherry

1 tablespoon minced fresh ginger

2 garlic cloves, crushed under a knife

¼ teaspoon Chinese chili paste with garlic

MAKES ABOUT 1 2/3 CUPS, ENOUGH FOR 2 POUNDS SHRIMP

2 tablespoons kosher salt

2 tablespoons sugar

1 teaspoon whole black peppercorns, crushed in a mortar or under a heavy skillet

2 pounds extra-large shrimp, peeled with the tail segment left on and deveined

2 cups mesquite, soaked in water for 30 minutes and drained

1 bottle (12 ounces) lager beer

APPLE-MUSTARD DIP

½ cup high-quality apple butter (made from only apples and cider)

⅓ cup Dijon mustard

MAKES 4 SERVINGS

Mesquite-Smoked Shrimp with Apple-Mustard Dip

These shrimps are infused with the smoky-sweet flavor of mesquite, and can be used as an appetizer or main course or in salads like the Grilled Shrimp Caesar Salad (page 49). Some smoking methods can be accomplished indoors, but without a very strong hood ventilation system, the entire house ends up smoked, so I recommend doing all smoking outdoors. There is no need to go out and buy an expensive smoker—shrimp can be easily smoked in either a charcoal or gas grill. The recipe may seem long, but that's only because I have made it detailed for cooks who may not be familiar with the indirect heat-smoking technique. For smoking, use extra-large shrimps (about 21 to 25 per pound) instead of the jumbo, which take too long to cook through. A quick brining discourages any bacteria from multiplying on the surface of the shrimps during the long cooking period. It also gives the shrimp a crisper texture.

IN A MEDIUM NONREACTIVE BOWL, mix 4 cups water, the salt, sugar, and peppercorns to dissolve the salt and sugar. Add the shrimp. Cover and refrigerate, stirring occasionally, for 30 minutes. Drain, rinse under cold water, and pat dry with paper towels.

MEANWHILE, BUILD A CHARCOAL FIRE (use about 30 briquets) on 1 side of the bottom of an outdoor grill and let it burn until the coals are covered with white ash. Place an inexpensive aluminum pan on the bottom of the charcoal grate, opposite the coals. (If using a gas grill, preheat 1 side to Low, leaving the other side off. If using a Weber gas grill, adjust the burners to Low-Off-Low. In either case, place the aluminum pan on the turned-off area of the heating element.) Pour the beer into the pan. Lightly oil the rack.

SPRINKLE A HANDFUL OF THE WOOD CHIPS over the coals. (If using a gas grill, place the chips in a metal wood-chip holder and use according to the manufacturer's instructions.) Place the shrimps on the side of the rack over the pan and cover. Smoke the shrimps, without turning, until firm and opaque throughout, 45 minutes to 1 hour. The interior temperature of the grill should be 200° to 225° F. If your grill doesn't have a thermometer in the lid, place an oven thermometer next to the shrimp. Every 15 minutes, quickly sprinkle another handful of the drained wood chips over the coals. Do not open the lid more often, or the heat will escape.

TO MAKE THE DIP, combine the apple butter and mustard in a small bowl. Let stand at room temperature for at least 30 minutes to blend the flavors. Serve the shrimps hot, warm, or at room temperature with the dip on the side.

Bacon-Wrapped Shrimp with Quick Béarnaise Sauce

QUICK BÉARNAISE SAUCE

½ cup mayonnaise

1 tablespoon minced shallots

2 teaspoons chopped fresh tarragon
  or 1 teaspoon dried tarragon

1 teaspoon tarragon or red wine vinegar

⅛ teaspoon freshly ground white pepper

16 colossal shrimp, peeled with the tail
   segment left on and deveined

8 strips of bacon, cut crosswise in half

16 wooden toothpicks, soaked in water
   for 30 minutes and drained

MAKES 4 SERVINGS

My friend, Vicki Caparulo, is a well-known cooking teacher whose recipes are packed with flavor. Wrapping peeled shrimp in bacon helps keep it moist, but this is not a method for calorie counters. Nonetheless, these shrimps are the way to go when taste is more important than fat grams.

TO MAKE THE SAUCE, combine the ingredients in a small bowl. Cover and let stand at room temperature to blend the flavors, at least 1 hour. (The dip can be prepared up to 1 day ahead, covered, and refrigerated. Remove from the refrigerator 1 hour before serving.)

BUILD A CHARCOAL FIRE in an outdoor grill and let burn until the coals are covered with white ash. (If using a gas grill, preheat on High.) Lightly oil the rack.

WRAP A BACON STRIP AROUND EACH SHRIMP, securing the bacon with a toothpick. Grill, covered, turning once, until the bacon is crisp and the shrimp is firm, about 8 minutes. (If the shrimps seem to be cooking too quickly, move to a cooler part of the grill not directly over the coals.) Remove the toothpicks and serve immediately, with the sauce passed on the side.

Grilled Shrimp, Sage, and Pancetta Spedini

What we call kebabs, Italians call *spedini*. Marinated in sage and olive oil, then wrapped in Italian bacon, these shrimp *spedini* have a smoky, herby aroma that guarantees raves.

IN A MEDIUM BOWL, combine the oil, sage, garlic, and pepper. Add the shrimp and toss. Cover and refrigerate for at least 1 hour and up to 8 hours.

BUILD A CHARCOAL FIRE in an outdoor grill and let burn until the coals are covered with white ash. (If using a gas grill, preheat on High.) Lightly oil the rack.

REMOVE THE SHRIMP FROM from the marinade. Wrap each shrimp in a piece of pancetta. Using 2 parallel skewers for 4 shrimps, thread the shrimps onto the skewers, piercing each one through the top and bottom so it keeps its natural curve. Grill the *spedini*, covered, turning once, until the pancetta is crisp and the shrimp is firm, about 8 minutes. (If the shrimps seem to be cooking too quickly, move to a cooler part of the grill not directly over the coals.) Remove from the skewers and serve immediately.

⅓ cup extra virgin olive oil

2 tablespoons finely chopped fresh sage

1 garlic clove, crushed through a press

¼ teaspoon freshly ground pepper

16 colossal shrimp, peeled with the tail left on and deveined

8 slices Italian pancetta, uncurled and cut crosswise in half

8 bamboo skewers, soaked in water for 30 minutes and drained

MAKES 4 SERVINGS

Shrimp from the Oven

Baked Artichokes with Basil Shrimp Stuffing
Oven-Barbecued Shrimp
Savory Shrimp Bread Pudding
Baked Shrimp with Catfish Stuffing
El Paso–Style Stacked Shrimp Enchiladas
Shrimp with Feta Cheese Taverna
Baked Shrimp with Herbed Crumb Topping
Quick Crumbed Shrimp with Mustard Sauce
Baked Shrimp with Roasted Garlic–Lemon Sauce
Scampi Classico
Shrimp Pan Pizza with Fontina Cheese and Asparagus

**BAKED ARTICHOKES WITH BASIL
SHRIMP STUFFING**

6 medium (8 ounces *each*) artichokes, stems cut off and discarded

1 lemon, cut in half

¼ cup extra virgin olive oil

¼ cup minced shallots or scallions, white parts only

1 garlic clove, minced

1 pound medium shrimp, peeled and deveined (page 17)

1½ cups soft bread crumbs

⅓ cup freshly grated Parmesan cheese

3 tablespoons chopped fresh basil

1 large egg, beaten

¼ teaspoon salt

¼ teaspoon freshly ground pepper

2 cups chicken broth, preferably homemade, or use low-sodium canned broth

MAKES 6 SERVINGS

Baked Artichokes with Basil Shrimp Stuffing

These stuffed artichokes are a delicious supper dish, served with just a tossed green salad on the side.

BRING A LARGE POT OF LIGHTLY SALTED WATER TO A BOIL over high heat. Cut off the top inch from each artichoke, rubbing the cut area with a lemon half. Squeeze the lemons into the water. Add the artichokes and cover. Cook until the artichokes are barely tender, 20 to 25 minutes. Drain the artichokes and rinse under cold water until cool enough to handle. Hold an artichoke, cut side down, and squeeze gently to remove excess water. Pull out the center leaves to reveal the hairy choke. Scrape out the choke with the tip of a spoon. Repeat with the remaining artichokes.

IN A MEDIUM SKILLET, heat 1 tablespoon of the oil over medium heat. Add the shallots and garlic. Cook, stirring occasionally, until the shallots are softened, about 2 minutes. Add the shrimp and cook until pink and firm, 1 to 2 minutes. Transfer to a large bowl. Add the bread crumbs, Parmesan, basil, egg, salt, and pepper and mix well. Stuff the artichokes with the shrimp mixture.

POSITION A RACK IN THE TOP THIRD OF THE OVEN and preheat to 400° F.

PLACE THE ARTICHOKES in a baking dish just large enough to hold them snugly. Brush the outsides of the artichokes with the remaining 3 tablespoons of oil and drizzle any oil left over the stuffing. Pour in the broth and cover tightly with foil. Bake for 15 minutes. Uncover and continue baking until the stuffing is heated through, about 10 minutes more. To serve, place each artichoke in a soup bowl and ladle the broth around the artichokes.

Oven-Barbecued Shrimp

Any time shrimp is baked in the shell in a sauce in New Orleans, it is called "barbecued," regardless of what is in the sauce or of the fact that this dish is not cooked outdoors. This version is especially delicious, with butter playing a large role in making a smooth, delectable sauce.

PREHEAT THE OVEN TO 425° F.

PLACE THE SHRIMP in a glass or ceramic 15 x 10-inch (4-quart) baking dish. In a medium skillet, heat 2 tablespoons of the butter over medium heat. Add the onion and celery. Cook, stirring often, until the onion is golden, about 4 minutes. Add the garlic and stir until fragrant, about 1 minute. Stir in the Cajun Seasoning, then the catsup and Worcestershire and bring to a simmer. Remove from the heat. Whisk in the remaining 10 tablespoons butter, 1 tablespoon at a time. Pour the sauce over the shrimp and toss.

BAKE, STIRRING OCCASIONALLY, just until the shrimps are pink and firm, 15 to 20 minutes. Serve immediately, with plenty of napkins alongside.

12 tablespoons (1½ sticks) unsalted butter, cut into pieces, chilled

1 medium onion, finely chopped

1 medium celery rib with leaves, finely chopped

2 garlic cloves, minced

1 tablespoon Cajun Seasoning (page 71)

¼ cup catsup

3 tablespoons Worcestershire sauce

2 pounds large shrimp

MAKES 4 SERVINGS

2 tablespoons unsalted butter

2 large eggs

1⅓ cups heavy cream

3 tablespoons dry sherry

2 teaspoons Worcestershire sauce

¼ teaspoon celery seeds

¼ teaspoon salt

⅛ teaspoon cayenne

2 scallions, white and green parts, finely chopped

8 slices firm sandwich bread, including crusts, cut into ¾-inch squares

1 pound medium shrimp, peeled and deveined

MAKES 4 TO 6 SERVINGS

Savory Shrimp Bread Pudding

Recipes for savory bread pudding abound in old Southern cookbooks. As the pudding itself doesn't include any vegetables, serve an asparagus and mushrooms sauté as a side dish.

POSITION A RACK in the center of the oven and preheat to 400° F. Generously coat the sides and bottom of a 13 x 9-inch (3-quart) glass baking dish with 1 tablespoon of the butter.

IN A MEDIUM BOWL, whisk the eggs. Gradually whisk in the heavy cream, then the sherry, Worcestershire, celery seeds, salt, and cayenne. Stir in the scallions. Spread half of the bread in the baking dish. Arrange the shrimp in a single layer on top, then cover with the remaining bread. Slowly pour the egg mixture into the dish to evenly moisten the bread. Let stand for 5 minutes. Dot the top with the remaining 1 tablespoon butter.

BAKE FOR 5 MINUTES. Reduce the oven temperature to 350° F. Continue baking until a knife inserted about 1 inch from the center comes out clean, 20 to 25 minutes. Let stand for 5 minutes before serving.

Baked Shrimp with Catfish Stuffing

Farm-raised catfish has a mild flavor and gelatinous texture that make it perfect for turning into a mousse-like stuffing for jumbo shrimp. The shrimp can be stuffed well ahead of baking and only need a quick trip to the oven before serving.

POSITION A RACK in the top third of the oven and preheat to 375° F. Lightly butter a 15 x 10-inch (4-quart) glass baking dish.

BUTTERFLY EACH SHRIMP by deepening the deveining incision with a small sharp knife, reaching almost, but not all the way, through the shrimp, and spreading it open. Arrange the butterflied shrimps side-by-side in the baking dish, alternating the directions of the tails.

IN A SMALL BOWL, soak ¼ cup of the bread crumbs in the heavy cream for 5 minutes. In a food processor, process the catfish, soaked bread crumbs and cream, egg white, tarragon, salt, and hot pepper sauce until smooth. Place about 1 tablespoon of the catfish stuffing on each shrimp, forming into a oval mound. (The shrimp can be stuffed 4 hours ahead, covered, and refrigerated. Remove from the refrigerator 30 minutes before baking.)

SPRINKLE THE TOPS OF THE STUFFED SHRIMPS with the remaining 2 tablespoons bread crumbs and dot with 2 tablespoons of the butter. Pour the wine around the shrimps. Bake, uncovered, until the tops are lightly browned and the stuffing is firm, 15 to 20 minutes.

TRANSFER THE SHRIMPS to dinner plates. Whisk the remaining 2 tablespoons of butter and the lemon juice into the cooking juices in the baking dish. Season with salt and pepper as needed. Pour the sauce around the shrimp and serve immediately.

16 colossal shrimp, peeled with the tail segment left on and deveined

¼ cup plus 2 tablespoons fresh bread crumbs

2 tablespoons heavy cream

8 ounces skinless catfish fillets, cut into 1-inch pieces

1 large egg white

½ teaspoon minced fresh tarragon or ¼ teaspoon dried tarragon

¼ teaspoon salt, plus more to taste

⅛ teaspoon hot pepper sauce, plus more to taste

¼ cup (½ stick) unsalted butter, cut into small pieces

⅓ cup dry white wine

1 teaspoon fresh lemon juice

Freshly ground pepper, to taste

MAKES 4 SERVINGS

El Paso–Style Stacked Shrimp Enchiladas

Whenever I go to El Paso, my friend Park Kerr takes me to a great Mexican food joint attached to a car wash, where we get stacks of enchiladas for breakfast. That's right, not pancakes but enchiladas, truly the breakfast of champions. These stacked enchiladas are fun to make. While we have to substitute feta cheese for the sharp Mexican cheese that is not imported into this country, the rust-red, dried chile enchilada sauce is as authentic as it gets.

TO MAKE THE SAUCE, place the chiles in a medium bowl and add the boiling broth. Cover with a plate and let stand, stirring occasionally, until the chiles soften, about 20 minutes.

MEANWHILE, HEAT THE OIL in a medium nonstick skillet over medium heat. Add the onion and cook, stirring occasionally, until golden brown, about 6 minutes. Add the garlic and stir for 1 minute. Sprinkle with the flour, oregano, and salt and reduce the heat to low. Stir for 1 minute. Transfer to a blender or a food processor.

DRAIN THE CHILES in a wire sieve, reserving the broth. Place the chiles in the blender and pour in 1 cup of the broth. With the machine running, gradually pour in the remaining broth until the sauce is smooth. (The sauce can be prepared up to 2 days ahead, cooled, covered, and refrigerated. Reheat before using. If the reheated sauce is thicker than heavy cream, thin with additional broth.) Pour the sauce into the skillet and bring to a bare simmer over low heat.

(CONTINUED)

ENCHILADA SAUCE

- 10 dried mild New Mexican chile peppers, rinsed under cold water, stemmed, seeded, and torn into pieces (see Note)
- 3 cups chicken broth, preferably home-made, or use low-sodium canned broth, heated to boiling
- 2 tablespoons olive oil
- 1 medium onion, chopped
- 2 large garlic cloves, minced
- 2 tablespoons all-purpose flour
- 1½ teaspoons dried oregano
- ½ teaspoon salt

- 1 tablespoon olive oil, plus additional for the baking sheet
- 1 pound medium shrimp, peeled, deveined, and coarsely chopped
- 12 corn tortillas (8 inches)
- 4 ounces feta cheese, crumbled
- ¼ cup freshly grated Parmesan cheese

MAKES 4 SERVINGS

IN A LARGE (12-INCH) SKILLET, HEAT THE OIL over medium-high heat. Add the shrimp and cook, stirring occasionally, until pink and firm, about 2 minutes. Set aside.

PREHEAT THE OVEN TO 400° F. Lightly oil a large baking sheet.

USING TONGS, dip a tortilla into the simmering sauce. Transfer to the baking sheet. Repeat with 3 more tortillas, placing them as far apart as possible on the baking sheet. Sprinkle the tortillas with half of the shrimp, then half of the feta. Repeat the dipping procedure with 4 more tortillas, placing 1 tortilla on top of each stack and sprinkling with shrimp and feta. Dip the remaining 4 tortillas in the sauce, and place them on tops of stacks. Sprinkle each stack with 1 tablespoon of the Parmesan. Keep the remaining sauce warm.

BAKE UNTIL THE PARMESAN IS MELTED and the tortillas are heated through, about 5 minutes. Using a wide spatula, transfer each stack to a dinner plate. Serve immediately, spooning the remaining sauce onto the plates.

NOTE: New Mexican chiles are available at Mexican markets, specialty food stores, many supermarkets, and by mail order (page 161). They come mild, medium-hot, and hot, so read the label carefully. You may use the hot chiles, if you prefer.

Shrimp with Feta Cheese Taverna

A taverna is the Greek equivalent of the Italian trattoria, a casual restaurant serving the best in delicious, unpretentious food. This dish is found on just about every taverna menu. Serve it with rice or orzo, the rice-shaped pasta.

IN A LARGE SKILLET, heat 2 tablespoons of the oil over medium heat. Add the onion and cook until golden, about 4 minutes. Add the garlic and cook for 1 minute. Add the wine and boil over high heat until reduced to about 3 tablespoons. Stir in the tomatoes with their juice, the basil, oregano, and red pepper. Bring to a simmer and reduce the heat to medium-low. Cook, stirring occasionally, until the juices are thickened, 20 to 25 minutes.

PREHEAT THE OVEN TO 400° F.

TRANSFER THE SAUCE to a shallow 2-quart baking dish. Stir in the shrimp. Sprinkle with the feta, then the bread crumbs and drizzle with the remaining 1 tablespoon oil. Bake until the shrimps are pink and firm, about 15 minutes. Serve from the baking dish, spooned over the orzo.

3 tablespoons extra virgin olive oil

1 medium onion, chopped

2 garlic cloves, minced

½ cup dry white wine or vermouth

1 can (28 ounces) peeled plum tomatoes in juice, juices reserved, chopped

1 teaspoon dried basil

1 teaspoon dried oregano

¼ teaspoon crushed red pepper

1½ pounds large shrimp, peeled and deveined

4 ounces feta cheese, crumbled

¾ cup fresh bread crumbs, toasted (see page 104)

Hot cooked rice or orzo, for serving

MAKES 4 TO 6 SERVINGS

Baked Shrimp with Herbed Crumb Topping

10 tablespoons (1 stick plus 2 tablespoons) unsalted butter, at room temperature

1½ cups fresh bread crumbs

2 tablespoons minced shallots

3 tablespoons chopped fresh parsley or ¼ cup if using dried herbs

2 teaspoons chopped fresh tarragon or 1 teaspoon dried tarragon

2 teaspoons chopped fresh thyme or 1 teaspoon dried thyme

2 teaspoons minced fresh basil or 1 teaspoon dried basil

2 pounds extra-large shrimp, peeled and deveined

½ cup dry vermouth

¼ teaspoon salt

¼ teaspoon freshly ground pepper

MAKES 4 SERVINGS

Shrimp de Jonghe was named for a Belgian family who ran a fine restaurant on Chicago's South Side. Unfortunately, many imitations marred by overbaked shrimp and soggy topping ruined its reputation, but this recipe returns it to the pantheon of twentieth-century American cooking, especially when it is cooked with garden-fresh herbs. Traditionally, Shrimpe de Jonghe was baked in individual gratin dishes, but not many cooks have them. Just bake the shrimp in a large dish and serve with plenty of good bread for dipping into the herby juices.

POSITION A RACK in the top of the oven and preheat to 450° F. Generously coat the inside of a 15 x 10-inch (4 quart) glass baking dish with 2 tablespoons of the butter.

IN A FOOD PROCESSOR, process the remaining 8 tablespoons butter with the bread crumbs, shallots, parsley, tarragon, thyme, and basil until well combined.

ARRANGE THE SHRIMP IN THE BAKING DISH in a single layer. Pour the vermouth over the shrimps and season with the salt and pepper. Crumble the herbed bread mixture on top.

BAKE UNTIL THE SHRIMPS ARE PINK AND FIRM and the topping is lightly browned, 8 to 12 minutes. Let stand for 2 minutes. Serve the shrimps, with the juices, in soup bowls.

Quick Crumbed Shrimp with Mustard Sauce

This recipe is based on a favorite of my colleague Dixie Blake, one of the people at Ocean Garden Products, the largest purveyor of fine Mexican Gulf shrimp. It makes a quick, elegant supper to serve with rice and steamed asparagus.

TO MAKE THE SAUCE, in a medium nonreactive saucepan, bring the wine to a boil over medium heat. In a small bowl, whisk the cornstarch into the heavy cream. Add to the wine and bring to a simmer. Cook until slightly thickened, about 1 minute. Remove from the heat, whisk in the mustard, turmeric, salt, and pepper. (The sauce can be prepared up to 2 hours ahead and kept at room temperature. Reheat gently before serving.)

POSITION A RACK in the top third of the oven and preheat to 500° F. Lightly oil a jelly-roll pan.

IN A SMALL SAUCEPAN, melt the butter with the oil. Transfer to a small bowl and set aside.

IN A MEDIUM BOWL, mix the bread crumbs, chives, parsley, oregano, and basil. Dip the shrimps one at a time in the melted butter, then coat with the herbed bread crumbs. Place on the pan. Drizzle the shrimps with any of the remaining butter-oil mixture.

BAKE UNTIL THE CRUMBS ARE LIGHTLY BROWNED, about 7 minutes. To serve, spoon some sauce onto each of 4 dinner plates. Arrange the shrimps on top of the sauce and serve immediately.

MUSTARD SAUCE

½ cup dry white wine

1 teaspoon cornstarch

⅔ cup heavy cream

2 tablespoons Dijon mustard

⅛ teaspoon turmeric

Scant ½ teaspoon salt

¼ teaspoon freshly ground pepper

4 tablespoons (½ stick) unsalted butter, melted

¼ cup extra virgin olive oil, plus more for pan

1 cup dried bread crumbs

1 tablespoon minced fresh chives

1 tablespoon minced fresh parsley

½ teaspoon dried oregano

½ teaspoon dried basil

1½ pounds large shrimp, peeled with the tail segment left on and deveined

MAKES 4 SERVINGS

5 tablespoons unsalted butter, cut up

¼ cup extra virgin olive oil

⅓ cup mashed Roasted Garlic
(recipe follows)

3 tablespoons fresh lemon juice

2 tablespoons chopped fresh parsley

1 teaspoon chopped fresh thyme or
½ teaspoon dried thyme

Grated zest of 1 lemon

¼ teaspoon salt

¾ teaspoon freshly ground pepper

2 pounds large shrimp, peeled with the
tail segments left on and deveined

MAKES 4 SERVINGS

Baked Shrimp with Roasted Garlic–Lemon Sauce

Whenever I teach cooking classes in San Francisco, Laura Gates is by my side, chopping and cleaning and telling jokes. Her California-style version of shrimp scampi uses roasted garlic and extra virgin olive oil, which create a sauce that is made to be sopped up with sourdough bread.

POSITION A RACK in the top third of the oven and preheat to 500° F.

STIR ALL OF THE INGREDIENTS except the shrimp in a 15 x 10-inch (4-quart) glass or ceramic baking dish. Add the shrimp and toss well.

BAKE, STIRRING OCCASIONALLY, until the shrimps are pink and firm, about 10 minutes. Serve immediately.

Roasted Garlic

Preheat the oven to 350° F. Cut each of 2 heads of unpeeled plump garlic horizontally in half. Drizzle each cut surface with a few drops of extra virgin olive oil and put the 2 halves of each head back together so as to reform the original heads. Wrap each head tightly in foil. Place on a baking sheet. Bake until the garlic feels soft when squeezed, about 40 minutes. Unwrap and cool until easy to handle. Squeeze the softened flesh from the hulls into a small bowl, discarding the hulls. Using a fork, coarsely mash the garlic pulp. Makes about ⅓ cup. (The roasted garlic can be prepared up to 1 day ahead, covered, and refrigerated.)

Scampi Classico

Scampi is the Venetian word for Dublin bay prawns, also known as langoustines. They look like baby lobsters with long, thin claws. You can simply use large shrimp, cooked in the classic style with parsley butter, lemon, and garlic.

POSITION A BROILER RACK 6 inches from the source of heat and preheat.

IN A HEATPROOF DISH large enough to hold the shrimp in 1 layer, toss the shrimp with the oil and set aside.

IN A MEDIUM BOWL, mash the butter, parsley, lemon juice, garlic, salt, and pepper with a rubber spatula until combined. Dot the shrimps with dollops of the butter.

BROIL, TURNING THE SHRIMPS ONCE, until the butter is sizzling and the shrimp is pink and firm, about 3 minutes. Serve immediately.

2 pounds large shrimp, peeled with the tail segment left on and deveined

1 tablespoon extra virgin olive oil

¾ cup (1½ sticks) unsalted butter, at room temperature

2 tablespoons chopped fresh parsley

2 tablespoons fresh lemon juice

2 garlic cloves, crushed through a press

¼ teaspoon salt

¼ teaspoon freshly ground pepper

MAKES 4 TO 6 SERVINGS

PIZZA DOUGH

2½ cups unbleached all-purpose flour

1 teaspoon quick-acting dry yeast

1 teaspoon salt

Pinch of sugar

1 cup hot tap water

2 tablespoons extra virgin olive oil, plus more for brushing

Cornmeal, for sprinkling

8 ounces thin asparagus spears, trimmed and cut into ½-inch pieces

2 tablespoons extra virgin olive oil

1 garlic clove, crushed through a press

2 cups (8 ounces) shredded Italian fontina cheese

¾ pound large shrimp, peeled, deveined, cut lengthwise in half, and patted dry

3 ripe plum tomatoes, seeded and cut into ½-inch dice

¼ teaspoon freshly ground pepper

2 tablespoons chopped fresh basil or marjoram or a combination

MAKES ONE 12-INCH PIZZA

Shrimp Pan Pizza with Fontina Cheese and Asparagus

You're unlikely to find this upscale flavor combination in your local pizzeria. I find it much easier to make homemade pizza in a rectangular pan, rather than fussing with baking stones and peels. Italian fontina cheese is better than the Swedish kind.

TO MAKE THE DOUGH, in a food processor, pulse the flour, yeast, salt, and sugar to mix. In a glass measuring cup, mix the hot water and oil. With the machine running, pour the liquid through the feed tube and process until the dough forms a ball. (If the dough feels too wet, add flour, 1 tablespoon at a time, and process until a ball forms. If it is dry and crumbly, add water, 1 tablespoon at a time.) Process the dough for 45 seconds longer. Remove the top of the food processor. Place a large piece of plastic wrap over the top of the work bowl, and reattach the top, making an airtight seal. Let stand for 10 minutes.

TRANSFER THE DOUGH to a large self-sealing plastic bag and seal the bag. Let stand in a warm place until the dough has doubled in bulk (a finger inserted ½ inch into the dough will leave an impression), about 45 minutes.

POSITION A RACK in the top third of the oven and preheat to 450° F. Sprinkle a thin layer of cornmeal over a 15 x 15 x 1-inch jelly-roll pan.

PAT AND STRETCH THE DOUGH into the pan. Cover with plastic wrap and let stand in a warm place until slightly puffy, about 15 minutes.

BRING A MEDIUM SAUCEPAN OF LIGHTLY SALTED WATER to a boil over high heat. Add the asparagus and cook until crisp-tender, about 2 minutes. Drain, rinse under cold water, and drain again. Pat dry and set aside.

IN A SMALL BOWL, combine the oil and garlic. Brush the dough with 1 tablespoon of the garlic oil. Sprinkle the dough with 1 cup of the fontina. Top with the shrimp, tomatoes, and remaining 1 cup cheese. Sprinkle with the pepper. Bake until the edges of the crust are beginning to brown, about 20 minutes.

TOSS THE ASPARAGUS with the remaining 1 tablespoon garlic oil. Scatter over the pizza, patting the asparagus lightly onto the top of the pizza so the pieces adhere to the cheese. Continue baking until the underside of the crust is golden brown (lift up with a spatula to check), about 5 minutes more. To serve, sprinkle with the basil and cut into large rectangles. Serve hot.

Mail-Order Sources

THE BAKER'S CATALOGUE
(King Arthur Flour)
P.O. Box 876
Norwich, VT 05055-0876
1-800-827-6836
White rice flour

MO HOTTA-MO BETTA
P.O. Box 4136
San Luis Obispo, CA 93403
1-800-462-3320 or 1-805-544-4051
Canned chipotles en adobo, New Mexican chiles

THE ORIENTAL PANTRY
423 Great Road
Acton, MA 01720
1-800-828-0368
Great source for Thai, Vietnamese, and Chinese
ingredients, including fresh lemongrass

Index

Table of Equivalents

The exact equivalents in the following tables have been rounded for convenience.

LIQUID AND DRY MEASURES

U.S.	METRIC
¼ teaspoon	1.25 milliliters
½ teaspoon	2.5 milliliters
1 teaspoon	5 milliliters
1 tablespoon (3 teaspoons)	15 milliliters
1 fluid ounce (2 tablespoons)	30 milliliters
¼ cup	60 milliliters
⅓ cup	80 milliliters
1 cup	240 milliliters
1 pint (2 cups)	480 milliliters
1 quart (4 cups, 32 ounces)	960 milliliters
1 gallon (4 quarts)	3.84 liters
1 ounce (by weight)	28 grams
1 pound	454 grams
2.2 pounds	1 kilogram

LENGTH MEASURES

U.S.	METRIC
⅛ inch	3 millimeters
¼ inch	6 millimeters
½ inch	12 millimeters
1 inch	2.5 centimeters

OVEN TEMPERATURES

FAHRENHEIT	CELSIUS	GAS
250	120	½
275	140	1
300	150	2
325	160	3
350	180	4
375	190	5
400	200	6
425	220	7
450	230	8
475	240	9
500	260	10